# SURVIVAL AND CONCERNS

## By

## Alice Vaeth

First published by AuthorHouse 04/24/04

ISBN: 1-4107-0099-2 (e-book)
ISBN: 1-4184-2635-0 (Paperback)
ISBN: 1-4184-2636-9 (Dust Jacket)

Library of Congress Control Number: 2002096367


This book is printed on acid free paper.


Printed in the United States of America
Bloomington, IN


Websites:   Adobe Acrobat Reader
                Amazon.com
                Books-a-Million.com
                eBookHome.com
                BookSite.com
                Powells.com
                www.authorhouse.com

# Contents

# DEDICATION

This book is dedicated to my wonderful children, John and Anna Marie, who are my precious jewels. To my dear mother who set an example of patience and decency in an economically-deprived household. To my older sister, Loretta, who has meant so much to me throughout my life and especially during my growing-up years. She is a wonderful human being. To my brother, Arthur, who gave so much of himself to help others including providing a home for my widowed mother. Also, to my many friends and colleagues who have meant so very much to me over the years.

# FOREWORD

Going through a period of survival energizes the thought process. So it was with me. The experiences of my survival provided the stimuli for concern about life, human relationships, and political impact.

Childhood experiences as well as those related to a difficult marriage provided the incentive for developing a concern about life and the intricacies of our experience in it. Struggle prompts concern and thereby becomes the seed of change.

Following a discussion of how I survived a difficult childhood and marriage, and experienced two successful careers, I lead you into a field of thought about matters which relate to issues of both personal and national concern. You'll find both informative and mentally stimulating.

Some of the figures I quote to make my points, you'll find shocking. But they tell the story and support the positions I take.

I believe you'll find yourself thinking about matters you haven't previously given much if any thought to. You'll probably change your mind about a number of things.

We do not live in isolation which would allow us to sit on the sidelines and let the world pass by. We must be active participants in national affairs for they affect us whether we contribute or not. Our overall mission: to make our world a better place in which to abide.

Come, take a walk with me. I think you'll find it an interesting, informative, and worthwhile journey.

# SURVIVAL

Living in Muncie, Indiana, a small town northeast of Indianapolis, is my first memory. Ours was a very modest home with hardly more than sidings and inner walls which my father built. It was at 2714 South Monroe Street and was close to a home we lived in temporarily on Vine Street while awaiting the finishing of the construction.

My mother gave me baths in a round metal washtub commonly used in those years for washing clothes. Today you might find one of those washtubs in an antique store.

We were poor foodwise and clotheswise but you'd never know it from my father's beautifully landscaped yard. He was very proud and particular about his yard. He planted flowers in beds laid out meticulously in colorful magnificent designs. One that stood out was a flower bed in the shape of a star.

My father built this house at 2714 South Monroe Street in Muncie, Indiana. This picture was taken many years after we moved away from Muncie. My father's beautiful yard and flower gardens were no longer there when I returned to take this picture. The house has since been demolished.

1

My parents, Leroy Lacey and Grace (Nee: Warren) Lacey

The city held a contest in which it selected the most beautifully landscaped yard. My father's yard won the prize.

I think my father had his priorities mixed up. That yard and our poverty, well, I often think about it and continue to not understand it.

My father kept me busy pulling dandelions and other weeds. His yard had to be perfect and I take credit for at the ages of 5, 6, and 7 helping him to keep it that way.

There was one particular weed that intrigued me. It had a several-inches-long disconnected part encased in a sheath. I marveled at how a two-part weed could exist as one. The only weed, and it is called a weed, that I knew the name of was the dandelion which I thought too pretty to destroy. But I had to obey my father's orders and pull them because they didn't fit into his landscaping.

I surely knew how to pull weeds. Child labor? You might call it that. Other kids were playing with dolls and toys while I was weeding my father's yard. I didn't miss dolls and toys because I didn't know what it was like to have them.

And, I don't resent having to pull those weeds and not having toys. I admit that I missed what probably most people would consider a normal childhood. Pulling those weeds was O.K. I just wish my father had loved me. But more of that later.

My father was 11 years older than my mother. They were married when my mother was only 15 years old. I and my older sister Loretta were both born while our mother was still in her teens.

My mother was meek to the nth degree. I loved her very much. Married to my father when she was only 15 years of age, she was more like one of us children than a mother and she continued to be such throughout my growing up.

3

When I was about 6 years old, early in the morning my father would have my sister, who was three years older than I, and me walk about a half mile up the road to a dairy farm to get milk. Maybe we got it cheaper if we walked to the dairy farm and brought it home ourselves. I don't know. On that early morning walk, there was a big dog that would always bark and frighten us. I don't think my sister and I should have had to take that walk to get milk. But when you're a little kid you do what your parents order you to do.

My parents took my sister and me to a large city pool in Heekin Park. Our parents sat on a bench beside the pool and my sister and I went in the pool. We were out to where the water was up to our necks and we couldn't swim. We were terrified trying to keep from going under and drowning. Neither my sister nor I remember our parents showing any interest in rescuing us.

A strange fellow saw us struggling to keep from going under. He rushed out into the water with all of his clothes on and rescued us. My sister and I are sure we would have drowned if it hadn't been for that fellow. He was a very special person in my life. Bless him wherever he is. He truly saved our lives.

Picture permission of Emmett Smelser, Publisher, The STAR PRESS, Muncie, Indiana.

Heekin Park in Muncie, Indiana, where my sister Loretta and I almost drowned while our parents sat on a park bench seemingly unconcerned.

In reminiscing, I wonder if there was some ulterior motive in our parents letting us go in the water when they knew how deep it was and we couldn't swim. Babies are so easy to conceive, replacements so easy to get. Was this philosophy in our parents' minds? I now wonder.

Before starting school my grandfather told me the school had a whipping machine and this frightened me. What does a whipping machine look like? I wondered. And, I thought, for what reasons would the whipping machine be used. I worried about whether the whipping machine would result in bleeding. Also, I thought my teacher might use the whipping machine if she didn't like me. Maybe she wouldn't like me because I had red hair. Scared? Yes. So, my grandfather, by telling me about a whipping machine, made me afraid to go to school.

5

I started school in the first grade at the Roosevelt Elementary School in Muncie. The school was located a few blocks from our home. There was no kindergarten. Thus, the reason for my starting school in the first grade.

What a relief when I found there was no such thing as a whipping machine. I was so relieved.

My teachers were wonderful caring persons. They didn't just teach from their mouths, they cared from their hearts. Children respected them, not just because they were teachers but because of the wonderful caring persons that they were.

When I was in second grade Miss Frye, my teacher, asked me to stay after school to clean the blackboard. It was customary for the teacher to ask a different student each day to do this. Miss Frye used the occasion to give me a pretty little dress and matching panties. They were so beautiful. My rags had told her a story. How I loved her for that. She was so wonderful to do that. That was a lesson in kindness over and above the school curriculum. That lesson would stay with me throughout my life and I would always find a secret pleasure in giving to others.

Roosevelt Elementary School in Muncie, Indiana, where in the 2nd Grade my teacher, Miss Frye, gave me a beautiful little dress and panties because she sensed I needed clothes.

I am forever putting a mental rose of appreciation and gratefulness on Miss Frye's grave wherever she lies in her eternal resting place as well as on the grave of that wonderful fellow who, with all his clothes on, went out into the water of the pool in Heekin Park and saved the lives of my sister and me.

The wonderful caring persons in our lives. As we travel into the future, we remember them and want to go back and thank them again and again for the kindnesses they bestowed upon us. But it becomes too late. So, in memory of them, we pass kindnesses on to others.

My father had the wanderlust. Muncie wouldn't be a place where I would grow up. In fact, from the time of my birth in Allegan on the west side of Michigan we had already lived in several towns before we had moved to Muncie where my memory begins.

I and my sister Loretta were both born while we lived on Ely Street in Allegan, a small town about 130 miles north of Chicago near

Lake Michigan. I am told that as a baby I was in a coma with typhoid fever.

My mother holding me. My sister, Loretta, is standing

I wish we had lived in Allegan long enough for me to get acquainted with the place of my birth. I did learn later in life from the Allegan Chamber of Commerce that Allegan lays claim to the Carnelian automobile which is described as a racy little chain drive car manufactured by Howard Blood in conjunction with Louis Chevrolet and that less than 20 of this automobile were manufactured before production ceased.

Soon after my birth we had moved from Allegan to Roanoke, Virginia, where we lived briefly before moving to Kalamazoo, Michigan. We lived in Kalamazoo for a short period before moving to Muncie where my first memory begins.

I mention these moves because they explain my father's on-the-road temperament. He truly had the wanderlust which was evident throughout my growing-up years.

After a short time in second grade in Muncie, my father had us on the train heading for Ft. Smith, Arkansas. I wish I had had an opportunity to get acquainted with Ft. Smith but we were out of there soon after arriving. My father for some reason unknown to me decided that we wouldn't remain there. I have only one memory of the city. I remember a delight in standing with one foot in Arkansas and the other foot in Oklahoma. What a silly thing to have been excited about. But childhood excitement is such as that. I can't say I've been in Oklahoma but I can always say I had one foot in the state.

There is one other thing I remember about while we were in Ft. Smith. My father mentioned moving to El Paso, Texas, but we didn't move to El Paso.

Instead we boarded the train for Springfield, Missouri, in the Ozark Mountains. Here we settled down in a concrete house on the north side of town in the area of Commercial Street and Calhoun Street. Our house was within walking distance of the York Elementary School where I was enrolled to finish second grade. Settle down? Make some friends? My father was studying the map and the train timetable. We would soon be on the train again.

We were in Springfield for such a short time that I only remember the concrete house we lived in, the York School, Commercial Street and Calhoun Street. I don't remember the name of my teacher or the names of any of the other students.

Where will I finish second grade? I wondered.

The train now took us to Adrian, Michigan, a neat little college town about 60 miles southwest of Detroit and about 35 miles northwest of Toledo, Ohio. I liked Adrian, its streets lined with old victorian homes and neatly landscaped yards. Away from the bustling crowds of the big cities, it enjoys a relaxed atmosphere.

*Alice Vaeth*

Ours was not one of those beautiful victorian homes. My father purchased a more modest home on Oak Street which was far from pretentious but provided a roof over our heads.

I was enrolled in second grade in the Jefferson Elementary School. After attending second grade in three states, Indiana, Missouri, and Michigan, I should have celebrated for having finally finished the grade.

The only student's name I remember during those first two years of school is John Haney and I don't remember which of those schools he attended.

I had loved all those train rides. Just like all kids I couldn't sit still. I'd run up and down the aisle. I'd sit by the window and read the name of each town as the train stopped at depot after depot to pick up and discharge passengers. I loved the sound of the train going clickety, clickety, click, click, click as it traveled down the railroad tracks.

But we were now in Adrian. Those train rides would be stored in my mind as happy memories. Not every kid has that much fun riding on a train before finishing second grade.

All those moves didn't bother me. What did bother me was my clothes which didn't measure up to that of my playmates. I'd have to wait for another time in my life when I could handle the clothes problem. At this point I had to wear what my parents provided me.

I realized that I was captive to my childhood and that I had to endure it. I was anxious to grow up and be in charge of my own life. It would seem like an eternity to grow up and I had no way of putting an accelerator on the clock.

Those early experiences embedded in me a spirit of individualism. Regardless of how the world whirled around me, the actions of others I encountered, the ugly words I heard, whatever they may have been about, I decided at that early age that I would personally determine the thinking and acting road of my own life. I would hold my head high and concentrate on being a decent person in all respects.

When I learned about death, that someday I would die, I decided that I wouldn't do anything that I would be ashamed of on my death bed.

Evil of any kind would be a no-no. I would be captain of my own ship. This would make me a happy person throughout my life for no matter the problems with which I would be confronted, I would get through the storms of their intrusion by staying on a steady course of knowing that I did nothing to invite the problems but that they were thrust upon me.

I would concentrate on overcoming problems, not brood over them. Whatever the present is, it is, and if it is not pleasant I would have to find an intelligent way out of it. I would be my own best friend and would pursue other friendships very carefully. I didn't need a lot of friends beside me at that point in my life. I was anxious for the door to open to adulthood and that was my focus.

Our house on Oak Street burned down. I was in school when it happened. I never knew how the fire started. My mother had been talking over the fence with a neighbor when the fire started.

Neighbors were kind enough to take us in for a period. How wonderful of them to do that. There is much appreciation in my heart for what those neighbors did.

We moved into a house on Beecher Street and lived there for a couple of years. This was a move without getting on a train. Wow! This was different.

My Aunt Betty, my father's sister, and my Uncle Jack lived in Romulus, Michigan in the Detroit area. They would invite me to visit them. I was about 8 years old. My father would put me on the train to go to visit with them. My Aunt Betty would meet me at the train station. Another train ride. Wow!!

Left to right: Aunt Betty Douglas, my father's sister, and
my paternal grandmother, Mary Lacey

There is one thing I remember about those visits. My Aunt Betty
told me that in washing dishes the crystal should be washed and dried
first, then the good china, then the silver, then the pots and pans and
whatever else.

At home we didn't have crystal, good china, and silverware but I
added this knowledge to other bits I gathered over my growing-up
years for application in my adult life, that adult life I was so anxious
to arrive at. These and many other things I should have been taught at
home but never were. But I put them on little shelves in my brain for
later retrieval.

On one of those visits, my Uncle Jack touched me in an inappropriate manner so I never went to visit them again.

During the summer my father would take me with him to a cherry orchard in Palmyra a short distance down the road in the direction of Toledo. We earned so much a basket for picking the cherries. I love cherries and ate quite a few while filling the baskets.

It was very hot weather while we picked those cherries. I put a cold cloth around my neck and this resulted in mastoiditis. My right cheek swelled from the inflammation. It was unbearably painful.

My father would have nothing to do with doctors. He thought they cost too much.

I think my father viewed me as too much of a burden. As a baby I had had typhoid fever and had been in a coma and now there was this mastoid problem with my face all swollen and me suffering with pain.

My father apparently viewed me as a medical expense that he didn't want to cope with.

Without my father's knowledge my mother took me to Dr. Esli T. Morden, an eye, ear, nose, and throat specialist. Dr. Morden sent me to Bixby Hospital where he performed a mastoidectomy.

Dr. Morden was so wonderful to me. He gave me a Bobbsey Twins book and some Norris chocolates. Dr. Morden is another angel in my life.

My roommate in the hospital was concerned that she hadn't made her bed and left things in order before whatever happened that sent her to the hospital. Her mentioning that instilled in me a lifelong concern that everything is in order before leaving home because who knows when one might end up being in the hospital.

I started fifth grade in the fall with a shaved head and a big wide white bandage around my head.

On follow-up visits to Dr. Morden, he would pull out the strip of gauze he had put in my ear and would put a new strip of gauze in. Inserting the gauze hurt, but pulling it out tickled.

2nd, 3rd, 4th, and beginning 5th grade in the Jefferson Elementary School were wonderful. My teachers: Miss Crowell, Miss LaFountain, and Miss Goodgie were really great. I loved each of them as well as the Principal, Miss Carriage.

My closest friends in the Jefferson Elementary School were Louise and Bernice. I would go to their homes but they didn't come to mine. My parents didn't provide a spirit of hospitality. Throughout my growing-up years I would never invite friends to my home.

Here I was beginning fifth grade in the Jefferson Elementary School and we were going to move again. Again?? Yes, again. My father bought a 40-acre farm in Cadmus, Michigan about 8 miles west of Adrian.

Cadmus is a small crossroads town, hardly a town at all, more like an intersection surrounded by farms.

In the farmhouse there was neither plumbing nor electricity. There was no telephone. It was another place to exist without normal conveniences.

On the farm there were many black walnut trees. It was the fall of the year and many walnuts were lying on the ground with their green-turning-black casings. I'd use a hammer to crack them open, sit on the ground and enjoy my little feast.

I liked the little two-room schoolhouse in Cadmus. In one room a teacher taught Grades 1 through 6 and in the other room the teacher taught Grades 7 through 12.

2-room School in Cadmus, Michigan where I attended part of the 5<sup>th</sup> Grade.

My teacher was so nice to me. Come to think about it, all my teachers had been nice to me. Anyway, my teacher at this school liked my penmanship (the Palmer Method). She had me write some personal notes for her for which she gave me the language. I loved that.

I wore black bloomers and a middy blouse much of the time. Black bloomers were popular at the time. There should be one of those black bloomers in the Smithsonian Institution. But then, I guess not, there have been so many changes in clothing style over the years. The Smithsonian could hardly accommodate all of them.

Walking to and from school was the most difficult part of living on the farm. It was a blizzardy cold winter while we lived there. My skinny little body would wrestle with the wind while walking the 2½ miles to school and 2½ miles back home in deep and drifted snow. If students had been excused from school because of the snow there would have been no school at all.

En route to and from school, I'd stop at farm houses along the way to defrost my nose and return some warmth to my hands and feet. The ladies in those farm houses got used to my rapping on their doors. They were very kind to me. I can't return the kindness to those ladies so I try to pass it on to others as I go through life.

We had two horses we named Mike and Jake, a Jersey cow and a flock of chickens. My sister milked the cow every morning before going to school. Bless her. I'm glad I didn't have to milk the cow. I don't think I could have done it. I don't remember my father ever asking me to milk the cow. For that I am thankful. Very thankful.

Sometimes on weekends my mother would hitch one of the horses to the buggy and she and I would go the 8 miles into the city where she'd tie the horse to a tree or something and we'd spend some time visiting with a friend of hers, a lady whose last name was Craig.

I marvel at not only my sister milking the cow but also my mother's ability to hitch the horse to the buggy. It wasn't in my blood to be a country girl. That's for sure.

You probably guessed it. We're going to move again. Before completing the fifth grade in this 2-room schoolhouse, my father sold the farm and we moved the eight miles back to Adrian.

I would finish the 5th Grade in a different school than the one I had attended before moving to the farm. I would now attend the new Lincoln Elementary School, so new I could smell the paint.

Picture taken by Mary Ann Ehinger

Lincoln Elementary School in Adrian, Michigan where I finished 5th Grade and then attended the 6th Grade.

Just as I had attended 2nd Grade in three different schools (in fact in 3 different states), I now attended 5th Grade in three different schools but in the same state.

Always moving. I think my father's primary interest in life was buying and selling real estate. They say home ownership is the American dream. It was certainly my father's dream, a dream that he realized many times.

There was never a mortgage. I am confident of this. Nor was there a lease. He always owned the home we lived in.[*]

Our home back in Adrian was a colonial located halfway down the one-block Bradish Street which ends at the Raisin River. Our house was at 820 Bradish Street.

---

[*] Except for some very brief times like in Muncie, Indiana awaiting my father's construction of our home at 2714 South Monroe Street when we lived temporarily in a house on Vine Street.

17

It was a modest home of probably the 1920s or earlier vintage. It had a front porch, a well, an outhouse, and a nice front, side, and backyard.

A cement walk led straight forward from the front porch to the street. There was a side door which opened to steps leading to where my father would soon plant a garden. On the other side of the house was a door leading to a well with a hand pump that provided our drinking water.

We cooked on a wood-fueled stove and ironed clothes by heating the iron on the stove. The house was wired for electricity but my father had the electricity cut off. We used kerosene lamps. There was a telephone but my father had it disconnected.

Even with everything it lacked there was something charming about this house. Of all the houses we ever lived in I liked this one the most.

Food was scarce as it had been in the past. We ate a lot of cornmeal mush and sardines. My mother dampened stale bread, seasoned it with sage, and fried it. She baked gems (I later learned that gems are muffins) and molasses cookies. We picked wild blackberries and strawberries. In season we ate vegetables from my father's garden.

There was never any liquor in our house. We couldn't afford soft drinks. And there was no smoking ever. We were just a surviving family with a roof over our heads but little food and almost empty clothes closets.

We went to church on Sunday and learned that if you do bad things you go to hell, and so we were good. There was no swearing in our home. We didn't even say damn.

My mother was an exceptionally patient person, long suffering and never complaining. My father would fuss at her and I'd wedge myself in between them and beg them not to argue. My father was the provoker and my mother was the passive self-protector. Meek and mild would describe my mother.

My older sister was my father's pet. This didn't bother me. For some reason unknown to me he didn't like me. In fact he would ultimately get rid of me. More of that later.

Did he not like me because of my bright red hair? I was different with my bright red hair. My father had a sister who had red hair and perhaps that could have had something to do with why he didn't like me. What? What? What could have been the reason? I'll always wonder.

I never asked my father why he didn't like me. I was silent about any problems while I was growing up. I just wanted and was anxious to get out of my childhood. Up and away from it. I had to be patient.

I don't recall ever having a conversation with my father, or for that matter with my mother. They were just there. I grew up under my own direction. I was influenced by the teachings in Church. I give a great deal of credit there for my staying on track. Whatever your religious learnings you can always use those learnings as a stabilizing influence.

I'll mention something that I purposely haven't discussed before. My parents had a total of thirteen children and four of them were born after I was 19 years old. We each grew up under our own direction. No parental guidance. No hugs and kisses.

This book is about me, not about my siblings except where I choose to mention them. So this is a story about my life only.

I was greatly influenced by my mother and older sister because of the angelic-like lives they led. But they gave me no guidance. I led myself through my growing-up years. Without question, I reared myself.

Understanding there was no way I could circumvent the difficult years of my childhood was paramount to my enduring it. I had a dream for my future, and that dream would carry me through the clouds of today to the sunshine of tomorrow.

Sometimes I'd sit in the swing on the front porch and admire the colorful leaves on the maple tree and the beautiful white flowers on the spirea bush while I surveyed my life, pondered about my life's road, where I had been and where I was going.

Sometimes I'd see a garter snake scooting around and under the front porch.

Some hot nights my older sister and I would go out on the front lawn, spread a blanket on the ground and sleep on it. Today, remembering the garter snake that would scoot around and under the front porch, I wonder why we ever chose to sleep on the front lawn. Today, being aware of so much crime, no one should ever sleep on their front lawn.

Sometimes I'd join kids down by the Raisin River. We'd sit and talk. Nothing of any consequence. Just get together and gab. I never discussed my home life or my father. This was always a very personal thing which I chose to deal with by myself alone. I would always deal with it by myself. My childhood was a period to tolerate until I would grow up and would be captain of my own ship.

There is never ever room for self-pity. The world is full of people who lost their grip on life and sank into an ocean of despair. I was determined that no matter what I would be patient until the time when I would reach adulthood and would be in charge of my own life. I wouldn't take time to sit by the road and brood while on my way to adulthood.

Someday, someday, I kept thinking throughout my childhood. Thank goodness childhood doesn't last forever. We enter the door to adulthood with a lasting view of our childhood. For too many of us the door to adulthood is an escape door.

I loved my mother very much. She was such a sweet little lady and so polite. She was born the daughter of Sam and Louise Warren. When she was just a young girl her mother left home, leaving her and her sister in the care of their father. And then she had married my father when she was only 15 years old. She and her sister Mamie, both deceased now, were two of the sweetest, kindest, most wonderful ladies I ever knew.

My mother's mother was Catholic and her father was Seventh Day Adventist. I always felt that the difference in their religions brought about their separation.

Left to right:  Aunt Mamie Lowell (my mother's sister) and my mother

My mother would go around the house singing her little songs of yesteryear. One she sang went like this:

> If the wind had only blown the other way,
> I might have been a single girl today.

> Instead of washing twins and triplets
> I'd be taking ocean diplets
> If the wind had only blown the other way.

Yes, if the wind had only blown the other way. But it didn't. How different it might have been for any of us if the wind had blown the other way. Each of us has to deal with what comes in our direction. Dealing with it intelligently is most important.

My mother was short, hardly five feet tall, quite the docile lady, and never one to raise her voice. She just existed and coped. No leadership in her personality, Her only role seemed, to me, to have babies, babies who would grow up without direction from parents.

Sometimes my mother would be sitting with a magazine reading love stories. I'd be going around the house dusting and putting things in their proper place. I was a stickler for neatness.

While my parents didn't really rear me, having just provided a roof over my head and enough food to keep me alive, my mother's patience and never showing anger did set an example for me and I tended to follow in that pattern, living a life of patience and refraining from anger.

There was a teensy-weensy bit of luxury in our otherwise starkly furnished home. I loved the figurine on a shelf in our living room.

Our furniture was sparse. However, in the living room of this house on Bradish Street there was a Victrola and classical records I played on it. There was Chopin's Barcarolle. Also a Concerto in B Flat Minor and a record of The Old Refrain. I played those records whenever I had an opportunity. In the silence of the night I can hear those melodies in my memory.

And, there was a piano. A piano? We could afford a piano? I never knew how we came upon that bit of luxury. My father must have bought it at a secondhand store unless it was given to him. Music found its way through the stress of poverty.

My mother played the piano by ear, not having taken a piano lesson in her life. She would play favorite tunes and there would be singing. My father had a good voice and had sung tenor in the Dekoven Male Chorus in Muncie, Indiana. My father was of English descent and my mother was of German descent.

My great Aunt Anna Gulbransen (my grandmother's sister on my father's side) and my Great Uncle Axel Gulbransen owned the Gulbransen Piano Company in Chicago, but ours was not one of their pianos.

We were the poor relatives. The Gulbransens were an inspiration to me. They were part of the family tree who had risen in the world of money. They had achieved. Maybe I too could make it up a ladder. I'd have to select a ladder then get to the bottom rung of it and start climbing. Someday. Someday.

There is a certain pleasure I get when I come upon a Gulbransen piano. A number of years ago I saw a Gulbransen piano in the St. Matthews Cathedral in downtown Washington, D.C., the cathedral where President John F. Kennedy's funeral was held. I've seen others over the years. Psychologically this is ego building by association.

I liked the house on Bradish Street. I hoped this would be our permanent home. I liked the Lincoln Elementary School and later the Junior High School. I liked Adrian. I hoped we wouldn't move from this house.

Walking to and from school, I would pass one of the city's parks which I would frequent now and then. In the park there was a drinking fountain by which hung an aluminum cup for public use and everyone used that cup for drinking. No thought was given to the passing of germs.

I look back on the use of that community cup and am sure that with today's concentration on sanitation that cup must have at sometime through the years been removed.

There was a man who moved into a house catercorner across the street from our house. He had rabbits and he invited me to come into his house to see the rabbits. I went in to see the rabbits. He put me on his lap which I instinctively knew wasn't proper. I managed to free myself and run home. The reason he had rabbits inside his house was, of course, so he could attract little girls like me. I didn't tell my parents. I just stayed away from him.

My father's garden was full of english peas, green beans, yellow wax beans, tomatoes, carrots, potatoes, lettuce and corn. My older sister would pick the potato bugs off the potatoes and I would hoe the rows and pull weeds. I was about 11 years old.

I would pick the vegetables and my father would fill quart baskets with them, put them in my little red wagon, and direct me to walk down Main Street, knock on doors, and sell them. I did this many times. He told me not to come home until I had sold all the vegetables in my little red wagon.

One night, which happened to be Halloween night, it had gotten dark and I was still rapping on doors trying to sell those vegetables. I was afraid to go home without selling them. One man opened his door, looked at me with my little red wagon, and slammed his door in my face. Maybe he thought I was hoping for a lot of Halloween candy because I had a wagon. He didn't give me a chance to ask him if he'd like to buy some vegetables. I broke into tears. I wanted to get those vegetables sold so I could go home and I wasn't going to get them sold if people were going to slam doors in my face.

I had to get those vegetables sold so I could go home and I stuck to it until I sold them.

My father wasn't interested in my well-being. He needed the money and sending me down the street to sell his vegetables was a means of getting it. While I think it was wrong for my father to force me, a little child, to stay out in the darkness of the night to sell his vegetables, I was learning stickability and perseverance.

When I was 12 years old my father took me downtown one Saturday night. We had come out of a J. C. Penney Store. All of a sudden my father wasn't with me. He had vanished. To this day I wonder how he did it, but he suddenly was gone, nowhere to be seen. He had disappeared. It was around 9:00 PM. It was dark. The store was closing. I was frightened. Finally a policeman drove me home. I ran upstairs and climbed in bed. My father came upstairs and beat me. I peed in bed I was so frightened.

Picture taken by Mary Ann Ehinger

It was in a second floor bedroom of this home in Adrian, Michigan where my father beat me when he had been unsuccessful in getting rid of me by leaving me, a little kid, stranded in the dark of the night on a downtown street.

There is no question but that my father took me downtown that Saturday night to get rid of me.

Oh well, I always thought, someday I'll be out of my father's house and I was more anxious than ever for that day. It would happen sooner than I thought.

My father was apparently sorry he hadn't succeeded in getting rid of me that Saturday night so he tried another way. My father and I were walking down Main Street one afternoon. He spotted two ladies chatting in front of a home. Complete strangers. He asked them if one of them would take me. One of them agreed to take me to live with her family. He had really, really, wanted to get rid of me and he finally succeeded. He got rid of me and my red hair.

I continue to wonder if my red hair is why he didn't like me. I can think of no other reason. Had there been some problem between him and his sister who had red hair? I never had an opportunity to talk with that particular sister so I'll never know.

So now I'm with this lady who agreed to take me. She takes me to her home on North Main Street a short distance from the downtown area. Her name is Lucille Bain. She was an angel to take me. Her husband's name is Peter Bain. They have a young son named Jimmy. They were so wonderful to take me into their home. It hurt me that I wasn't allowed to sit at the table with them. I was seated separately. This was very hurtful.

Peter Bain and son Jimmy

Lucille Bain and son Jimmy

I was 12 years old when I went to live with the Bain family. I had a few more years to go before I'd be on my own. Oh, what a glorious day that will be, I thought. I would be through the tunnel of turmoil of my growing up and the sun of survival would be there to shine on me.

The day I reached the age of 13 is very vivid in my mind. It was a milestone. I was so elated to finally at last be in my teens. Now I needed to get through my teenage years and shed the shackles of bondage to my parents. I still felt the bondage even though I wasn't living with my parents.

I was lucky. I didn't fall to pieces under the weight of my father's treatment of me. While enduring his meanness my ship of life was sailing towards the future, a future that I had to be patient to reach.

I don't regret having to sell those vegetables in my little red wagon because it taught me responsibility and I think it was a whole lot better way to spend my time than the way a lot of kids who get into trouble spend theirs. But I don't think I should have been told not to come home until I had sold all of the vegetables in my little red wagon.

And I don't think my father should have tried to get rid of me by leaving me, a kid, on a downtown street corner in the darkness of the night and then beating me when a policeman took me home. And I don't think he should have given me away to a strange lady on the street. He didn't know what kind of person she was and he didn't care. I was fortunate that she turned out to be a nice lady.

Men like my father should never have children. Hugs and kisses would have been nice but I can handle not having had them. I just wanted to be treated like a human being, not like something disposable that is thrown to the winds.

I questioned my existence. Why did I get on the road of life in the first place? I didn't decide to get on the road of life. I didn't select the road. I just found myself on it and found myself with the burden of dealing with it.

Is this fair? I don't think so. I think God, whoever God is, should have more carefully thought out His Creation Plan. He should have used a different set of blueprints.

As an egg in my mother's womb, if I had been given an opportunity to preview what life on earth would be like I might have taken a hike and let the sperm search elsewhere. But God's blueprints didn't give me an opportunity to make a choice as to whether or not I wanted to be born. He didn't endow me with a working brain until after the sperm captured me and led me to a life on earth. No opportunity to escape. This isn't fair.

Life begins with Mother Nature's trickery, her luring through an ecstatic experience the joining of the sexes. If Mother Nature (part of God's blueprints) had not made that experience so ecstatic I might not have been forced into this world. Yes, "forced" is the correct word. Without question, I was forced into this world just like everyone else is forced into this world.

Not one of us, not a single human being, asked to come into this world and become a population statistic.

I had no more power to stop from being born than I have to stop a tornado in its path. Being forced into this world was not fair. Furthermore, I had no choice as to the door through which I would enter this world. I had no satchel in hand containing provisions to meet my needs. I arrived naked and was at the mercy of others when I took my first breath. Thus, I began life's journey totally out of my own control. I was at the mercy of those two people who created me.

My father and mother were not capable of filling the role of parenthood emotionally or financially. But here I was. I would have to squeeze through the tunnel of childhood to adulthood bound by the circumstances in which I found myself. Each person has his or her own set of circumstances to live with while growing up. And, circumstances vary widely. We have to make do with what we are given.

I envied those who are born into wealth and in an atmosphere of love and kisses. But envy is not productive. I had to wait until I would grow up and make my own life. Childhood would take such a big chunk out of my life. It would have been so nice if I could have been born grown up. Thinking the impossible is a waste of time.

Populating the earth was more important in the Creator's mind than the quality of life of the billions of people who would become its inhabitants. According to the Bureau of the Census, our world population is about 6 billion and in the next 50 years is expected to approach 10 billion.

I'm sure that if I had known what lay ahead of me in my childhood I would have opted not to be born. But, again, God's blueprints didn't provide me with an opportunity to make that option.

It is not fair that there are those of us who are born into poverty. We struggle to get something out of life while those born to riches coast through life with everything at their fingertips.

We should all be born equal. We're not. God's blueprint isn't fair.

Concentrating on the negatives of the past is an exercise in futility. We can only move forward into the future of our lives. The past is but a springboard into the future.

I like the words of Joaquin Miller, the philosopher, who said: "...tomorrow the stone shall be rolled away, for the sunshine shall follow the rain."

The Stock Market crash on October 29, 1929, when I was 14 years of age, ushered in the Great Depression. I was still living with the Bain family.

Desperation reigned and extended its tentacles far and wide as mankind struggled to extricate himself from the impact of the Great Depression. Banks closed and people lost their money as a result. Millions of people were without work. The need to survive became the dominant thought of the day.

My father lost his job. Two years into the Great Depression he decided to move the family to Jacksonville, Florida and asked me if I wanted to go with them. This was strange after having gotten rid of me, but my father was a strange man, at least to me he was. Maybe not to other people or to other members of our family, but to me he was a strange man whom I never understood.

Maybe my father was afraid of being charged with abandoning me if I found out the family had gone and he hadn't told me. I don't know. I wonder. He had already abandoned me when he gave me away to the Bain family. Maybe he thought I would refuse to go.

I decided to go with the family to Florida. Why? I've never answered that question to my own satisfaction. Maybe because there was a sense of belonging because of blood ties to the family.

So, in October of 1931 it was off to Jacksonville, Florida on a Greyhound Bus. Mother and father and 8 children. And, my mother was pregnant with a ninth child.

My father put a tent in front of the house we moved to in Florida and I studied and slept in that tent. No room for me in the house. And, my mother would give birth to 5 more children.

I lived in the tent for a brief period. I ran an ad in the Jacksonville newspaper looking for a family to live with while attending high school. I received a favorable response to my ad from a Mrs. Barnes. So I moved in with the wonderful Barnes family and lived with them through my high school years. They were so wonderful to take me in and their home was so convenient to the Robert E. Lee High School that I was attending. Their home was on Belvedere Street and their backyard backed up to the High School which was on McDuff Avenue.

How can I ever repay the Barnes family as well as the Bain family back in Michigan? It's too late. But I will forever be grateful to them for their kindnesses.

I received my High School diploma and was very proud for having won an essay contest in my senior year.

I loved school from the very beginning in Muncie, Indiana.

It's like a learning train, I thought. I wanted to pile as much knowledge on my learning train as possible. And, I vowed to continue piling knowledge on my learning train throughout my life. The caboose to my learning train would be my death bed. But I won't think about that now.

My father came to my graduation, but I kept my distance. My mother was pregnant and about to give birth to twins so she didn't attend. Here I was graduating from high school and my mother was still having babies. A year later she would give birth to another set of twins. My father had a double interest in life, owning real estate and having babies.

Graduating from high school was a second milestone in my life, the first having been when I became 13 years of age.

I wish my mother could have come to my high school graduation. I dearly loved my mother because she was so totally pure in character. I'm sure she never committed a sin in her life. She and her sister, my Aunt Mamie Lowell who lived with my Uncle George Lowell in Mt. Morris near Flint, Michigan, were two angels.

My mother never guided me. She never gave me advice. Never. She just set an example of patience and coping. I never held it against her for not stepping in when my father treated me so unkindly when he beat me and when he gave me away because I realized she was powerless to do anything and her words would have had no effect on him. I do not hold my mother responsible for my father's sins. No one should ever be held responsible for someone else's sins.

Following high school graduation, I was university accepted. Attending the university, however, was completely out of the question. I couldn't afford it. I needed to find work and make some money. I would find a way to work and take courses too. This I was determined to do. Education must be obtained one way or another. There is never a time to stop learning. And, we may resort to any number of ways to acquire learning. Learning is more important than how it is obtained.

A college or university degree has its place in the representation of knowledge acquired but is not in itself a guarantee of capability. There are many great men who never had that piece of paper to neatly frame and hang on their wall for everyone to see.

Thomas Alva Edison had little formal education, yet he held many patents for his inventions.

*Alice Vaeth*

Abraham Lincoln was self-educated. He became one of Illinois' most prominent leaders and was elected to be President of the United States. The Lincoln Memorial is one of the largest memorials in our Nation's Capital.

Benjamin Franklin was self-taught. He was President of the Constitutional Convention and was a member of the Committee which drafted the Declaration of Independence. He also made contributions to scientific investigations.

Andrew Carnegie came to America at the age of 13. He worked as a messenger boy for the Ohio Telegraph Company. He rose from poverty and sold his interests in the U.S. Steel Corporation for $250,000,000.

Cornelius Vanderbilt was a poor boy and had little schooling. He ran a business ferrying passengers between Staten Island and Manhattan Island in New York City then became wealthy in the steamship and railroad empires.

Strength of character and a desire to succeed is what it's all about. The green light to go forward must be in place and the will to march in the direction of success must be activated. Without motivation one cannot expect to reach the realm of success.

Here I was, wanting to attend the university and there was no way I could do it. I thought of the song my mother used to sing: "If the wind had only blown the other way." But the wind didn't blow the other way and I have to cope with my own set of circumstances.

It would take one step at a time. I was determined to rise up and out of the poverty I had grown up with.

After high school graduation and leaving the Barnes family which had made a home for me during those years, I had begun living with a church family which had befriended me, Roy and Carrie Martin and their two children. They were so wonderful to ask me to come and live with them.

34

Me with children of Roy and Carrie Martin who took me into their home when I had none.

Incident to the Great Depression many work programs were established under the leadership of President Franklin D. Roosevelt. Those programs provided work in many areas of capability. Without those programs millions would have likely died of starvation. Those work programs literally saved the nation.

My first job involved sitting at a desk eight hours a day writing grocery orders for people who had been identified as needy. My immediate supervisor was a social worker, a lady whose last name was Stewart. In this job I was paid $12.00 a week.

My family with whom I didn't live needed money and I would give them what I could and take them food. After several months the grocery-writing job ended.

I was desperate for work. I had to have employment. I applied for another government job paying $14.00 a week and was told there was no vacancy but that when a vacancy occurred I would be considered for it.

I accompanied the husband of the family I was living with into town every day and went to the office where I had been told I would be considered for a job when a vacancy occurred. I sat in that office all day long, day after day, so that they wouldn't forget me.

I look back on that experience and wonder at their letting me sit there day after day doing nothing, just waiting for a job opening. But they did let me, and I did finally get a job in that office. My persistence paid off. After several months the work ended and I and the others were let go. I will forever thank the lady who let me sit there waiting for a job opening.

I continued to go downtown every day with the husband of the family I was living with. All day long, day after day, I would walk the streets rapping on office doors trying to find a job. But I never found one through those efforts.

Finally I landed a job as a clerk-stenographer with the Federal Theatre Project, a work program administered by the Works Progress Administration (WPA). My salary in this job was $16.00 a week. The Federal Theatre Project was set up to provide employment for thousands of actors and actresses across the nation as well as for those involved in playwriting and directing.

My coworkers in the Federal Theatre Project were really great. It was so wonderful working in that office.

While my work was in the office, just for the fun of it I would usher now and then at one of the Theatre productions. I worked very hard in the office, intent on making an impression on my superiors. They were wonderful to me.

It was now about three years since I had graduated from high school. The Great Depression was still with us.

The Federal Government announced that a Civil Service Examination would be conducted for positions in Washington, D.C. This was my big opportunity.

I took the exam and passed it. In the Civil Service Commission in Washington, D.C. there was a list of those who had passed the exam and the names appeared on the list according to scores so that the names of those who obtained the highest scores on the exam appeared at the top of the list.

I must have done very well because I soon received a telegram requesting me to report to the Navy Department on Constitution Avenue in Washington, D.C. What an exhilarating feeling. No one can understand how much the words in that telegram meant to me unless they had experienced my childhood. My whole life would change.

I would leave Jacksonville and not return until 35 years later after the twins had grown up, gotten married, had children of their own, and my father had died.

I lacked money for the bus fare to Washington. My supervisor in the office in which I worked in the Federal Theatre Project loaned me the necessary amount for the bus fare and I boarded a Greyhound Bus for Washington, D.C. I was off to another world, a totally different world. How wonderful.

Nothing did I know about what lay ahead for me, but one thing I knew is that it would be completely different from the life I had lived before this point in my life. I had survived. I and my red hair would go to the nation's capital.

This picture of me was taken during my High School years in Jacksonville, Florida.

Elwood R. Robinson, my supervisor in the Federal Theater Project where I worked in Jacksonville, Florida. He and his wife, Hope, standing beside him, loaned me the money for bus fare to go to Washington.

# FEDERAL GOVERNMENT CAREER, MARRIAGE, and FAMILY

Riding the Greyhound Bus to Washington was a trip to a completely different world. It was the most wonderful trip I will ever take in my life. All the glories of Italy, France, and England couldn't have provided the exhilaration of this trip for it was taking me to a future that I had for so long dreamed about and waited so long for.

En route to Washington, I enjoyed viewing the countryside and the towns and villages as we traveled northward. I did a lot of reminiscing. I thought about those train rides as a child and the trip to Jacksonville on a Greyhound Bus.

What a joyous and exhilerating feeling when I alighted the Greyhound Bus at its station then located on New York Avenue about three blocks east of the White House.

It was a beautiful Spring day, March 30, 1937. The famous cherry blossoms were in full bloom and flowers were everywhere.

This was the third milestone in my life. I had escaped from my father's territory.

Several days before having departed for Washington, Katherine Haight, who had befriended me in the Federal Theatre Project and who was familiar with Washington, took me to lunch and explained the street and avenue layout of Washington, how the circles are located where the streets and avenues converge, etc. She had suggested that when I arrive in Washington that I stay initially at the YWCA. I was so fortunate to have her as a friend. Her advice, especially about the YWCA, was so helpful. So I had made a reservation at the YWCA.

After spending a couple of nights at the YWCA, I moved to a boarding house which the YWCA recommended and which was located two blocks away.

The boarding house was at 824 Connecticut Avenue across the park (Lafayette Park) from the White House where the President of the United States resides.

How could this happen? Me? Me? Unbelievable. Here I was living across the park from the White House.

The boarding house was almost fully occupied, so I was lucky to get a room. Four stories high, no elevator, and my room was on the fourth floor. Good exercise. A young girl who was secretary to a congressman on Capitol Hill shared the room with me.

824 Connecticut Ave., N.W., the Boarding House across the Park from THE WHITE HOUSE where I lived most of my first year in Washington, D.C. This Boarding House was later torn down and a new structure is now on the site.

I closed the door on my growing-up years. They would be buried in the deepest caverns of my mind. They would be something I wouldn't talk about. They had been full of desperation and that was something I no longer wanted to deal with. So I put a smile on my face and moved forward with my life.

I would continue to aspire, taking one day at a time. No onrush because things don't happen immediately. I had gotten through my growing-up years and now I was at the beginning of my dream world.

Most of the girls in the boarding house had come to Washington not as political employees like my roommate but rather to work for the various government departments as a result of having passed a Civil Service Examination in their home state as I had.

At that time there were a number of such boarding houses in the downtown area of Washington which accommodated young government workers like myself. They were privately run and were set up for the sole purpose of accommodating us newcomers to the Washington scene. Those boarding houses were such a blessing to those of us who resided within their walls.

One of the girls in the boarding house, Josephine Byrum, asked me to go on a blind date with her, mine being the blind date. Such polished young men. Real gentlemen. We went out with them a number of times. They took us to the Congressional Country Club on River Road in Bethesda, a Washington suburb, for dinner and dancing. I had never had dancing lessons which I hardly need to mention considering the poverty in which I grew up. But I managed to pick up the steps.

How was I so fortunate to be one of this foursome? To have been taken to a country club just a few months after my arrival in Washington? But, I had thought I would fit into the Washington scene better than the one I had left behind. I had been forced into the life of my youth but now I had the freedom to make my own life. It was like being delivered from captivity.

The Navy Department, the place of my employment, was in its pre-Pentagon days and was located on Constitution Avenue on the Mall and backed up to the Lincoln Memorial and the Reflecting Pool.

The boarding house where I lived was just a few blocks from the Navy Department. Walking to my office, I would cross Lafayette

Park, pass the White House and the War Department (now the Eisenhower Executive Office Building) on Pennsylvania Avenue, make a left turn on 17th Street, pass the Corcoran Art Gallery, Constitution Hall, and the Pan American Union Building (now the Organization of American States). On my left was the Ellipse where the national Christmas tree is lit each year. I would make a right turn on Constitution Avenue and arrive at my office.

Here I was embarking on a Federal Government career. Actually, the Federal Theatre Project where I had been employed before departing for Washington was a Federal Government program and would be counted toward my Federal Government service incident to later retirement.

The Federal Theatre Project would soon experience its last curtain fall as the Great Depression was gradually fading into history. Now I would be working in a Federal Government position with a future.

My job in the Navy Department was as a clerk-stenographer in the Bureau of Navigation, Grade 2, $1,440 a year salary. $1,440 a year?? Well, it was adequate for those times. Room and Board (including two meals a day) was only $37.00 a month. Unbelievable. These figures reflect the economy in the Great Depression.

Washington is probably the visitors' center of the Nation. Sitting on the ground by the Reflecting Pool within view of the Lincoln Memorial, the Washington Monument towering over 500 feet into the sky, and the Capitol Building at the far east end of the Mall, I would eat my lunch.

While sitting there eating my lunch, I would reminisce about my childhood and dream about my future. I would watch the many visitors who wandered about and wonder what their life story might be, what problems they might have had in their life. They would spend their week or whatever visiting the numerous sites in the Nation's Capital and they would then be going home. I was so glad that I wouldn't be traveling in that direction.

I loved my work in the office and worked very hard trying to make an impression on my supervisor. Also, I was and still am a perfectionist. I'm not saying I'm perfect. I'm saying I try to be. What else can one do for no one is perfect.

Anyway, I worked very hard and was making the kind of impression on my supervisor that I wanted to.

I was confronted by one of the other girls in the office who said I was hurting the other girls by significantly exceeding their production. Well, now, I guess I was naive because it never occurred to me that I'd be hurting someone else by doing a good job. I certainly didn't want to hurt anyone else. So, I slowed down.

Should I or should I not have slowed down is a debatable question. It's a problem I've never solved.

The Navy Department occupied one of three long three-story buildings which had been built on the Mall as temporary buildings during World War I. These temporary buildings lacked the architectural grandeur of the Federal Government buildings located in the Federal Triangle which had been built in the 1920's farther up the Mall closer to the U.S. Capitol Building.

The Mall is a scenic area and those temporary buildings located on it were an eyesore.[*]

I didn't like working in a shabby building. I wanted to work in a building that I felt more befitted the Nation's Capital. Wanting something more grandiose after what my childhood had consisted of? Well, I did. My mind-set had always been on elegance. Remember the figurine on the shelf that I had loved as a child and the classical music I played on the Victrola.

---

[*] President Richard M. Nixon, during his administration, had those temporary buildings torn down.

43

After 9 months in the Navy Department, I transferred to the Internal Revenue Service* which is located in the Federal Triangle. It had a grand lobby and long impressive corridors.**

I took my Oath of Office in the Treasury Department within which the Internal Revenue Service functions. The Treasury Department is located next to the White House.

My transfer to the Internal Revenue Service was as a clerk-stenographer. Soon I was promoted to the position of Secretary to the head of the Division. His name was Garwin Davis. I enjoyed working for him. I did have to cope with his smoking a lot of cigars. He was snazzy looking. He wore spats.

He let me in on a little story about his childhood. He said his mother told him to go out and dig some potatoes to cook for dinner and instead of digging potatoes he went to the store and bought some.

Internal Revenue Service colleagues. We worked in different offices. I am front row on left.

---

* At that time it was called the Bureau of Internal Revenue, the name being later changed to Internal Revenue Service.
** In later years they ruined the corridors of this beautiful building by lowering the ceilings and painting the walls.

About the time I transferred to the Internal Revenue Service, I moved from the boarding house on Connecticut Avenue to an apartment at 1515 16th Street with three other girls.

16th Street had at one time been known as The Avenue of Presidents because it ends on the south at Lafayette Park and the White House.

We were a happy congenial foursome in this apartment. Kathryn Ulasich had come to Washington from the upper peninsula of Michigan, Alice Seppala was Finnish and had come from somewhere out in the States but I don't remember where, and Viola Loose had come from the middle west.

We took turns cooking and performing other household chores. Viola's idea of comfortable living was having things not exactly in place so that they looked used. I like things in their place and not strewn about. But I didn't quarrel about it. I figured people are different and we can't expect everyone to adhere to our sense of comfort in living. I accept others as I hope they will accept me. I enjoyed their friendship.

1515 16th Street, N.W. (across from the famous Foundry Methodist Church) where I shared an apartment with three friends.

Left to right: Kathryn Ulasich, Alice Seppala, Viola Loose, and me. We shared an apartment at 1515 16th Street, N.W.

In those days the streets were safe, at least 99% safer than we experience as we enter the 21st century.

After dinner we'd sometimes walk several blocks up 16th Street to the Mormon Church (none of us were Mormons) located at 16th Street and Harvard Street where we'd sit and listen to the wonderful organ music.

Sometimes we'd go to the highly respectable Miller Dance Hall at 18th Street and Columbia Road. Many young government employees would be on the dance floor. We'd dance to the wonderful tunes of yesteryear. A favorite was "Sweet Leilani."

There were times when we'd go to the Elks Club for dancing. And, there was Catholic sponsored dancing on N Street. I wasn't Catholic but that didn't matter.

Other times we'd go to a Watergate Concert down by the Potomac River in the vicinity where the Watergate complex of Nixon fame was later constructed. We'd sit on the ground and listen to the wonderful music.

On a number of occasions we attended a National Geographic Lecture in Constitution Hall.

And, we went out on dates. We were girls who believed that sex should wait until marriage. We were virgins. Sex before marriage was out of the question. Otherwise we would have been scorned and disgraced. We were morally correct.

Our apartment was across the street from the famous Foundry Methodist Church which I had begun attending. I became a member of the Spencerian Sunday School Class. We informally called the class the Spencerian Class because our Sunday School teacher's name was Evelyn Spencer. We members of the Spencerian Sunday School Class would get together once a month in the evening at one of our member's place of residence. We'd sip coffee, partake of the goodies, and chat.

On Tuesday nights young people of the church would get together for dancing in the Letts Building[*] next door to the church. On Tuesday afternoons before the dances several of us would meet in the church kitchen to prepare hors d'oeuvres for the evening. Watching over us at the dances would be our minister, Dr. Frederick Brown Harris. Dr. Harris later became Chaplain of the U.S. Senate.

I co-starred in a play put on by the Church's Theatrical Group. This was a great experience. Acting permits you to disappear into someone else's personality. It is sheer enjoyment.

In Play at Foundry Methodist Church. I am seated wearing tiara.
Alberta Philpott is standing

---

[*] The Letts Building was later torn down to make room for the Brueninger Education Building which was made a part of the church. Now Foundry's gothic stone facade faces an entire block on 16th Street.

Foundry Methodist Church has a wide spectrum of activities. It was great for me.

I enjoyed the friendship of the girls I was sharing an apartment with at 1515 16th Street but when our lease was up we decided to give up the apartment. I moved to a boarding house in the next block at 1407 16th Street. The owner owned three boarding houses in the same block. The occupants of all three boarding houses would go to the dining room of the home the owner owned at 1401 16th Street for breakfast and dinner.

Two girls in this boarding house invited me to join them in subletting an apartment over a place of business at 1611 Connecticut Avenue near Dupont Circle. We sublet the apartment for the summer while its occupant, a school teacher, went on a trip to Europe for her summer vacation. One of the girls I shared this apartment with was Adeline McIntyre. She was from Oregon and worked for the Interior Department. The other girl, Catherine Clonts, was from Oklahoma. She was secretary to a congressman on Capitol Hill.

1407 16th Street, N.W., a Boarding House to which I moved after apartment living at 1515 16th Street., N.W.

1611 Connecticut Avenue, N.W. where Catherine Clonts, Adeline McIntyre and I sublet a 2nd Floor apartment from a teacher on summer vacation.

Adeline McIntyre on left. I am on right.

Catherine Clonts on left. I am on right.

When the teacher returned in the fall and we gave up the apartment, I moved to a boarding house at 1325 16th Street in the block next to Scott Circle.

This house at 1325 16th Street had just been purchased and converted to a boarding house. It was an elegant home. There was a large oval room which had been used as a library by its previous owner and would now be used as a dining room. The home had an elevator with velvet covered seats. (an elevator?? with seats??) The new owner, in converting the home to a boarding house, had furnished it with all new furniture, all in good taste.

Left to right:  Dorothy Shaughnessy, Dorothy Munter, and me, roommates in this beautiful home at 1325 16th Street, N.W., which had been converted from a private residence to a Boarding House.

I am in checkered jacket on left-hand side in front of this home which had been converted from a private residence to a boarding house.  This beautiful home at 1325 16th Street, N.W. was later demolished and a hotel was built on the site.

It's sad that as boarding houses in downtown Washington faded into history this beautiful home was torn down and a hotel was built on the site.

During this time period I was invited to become a member of the Kappa Gamma National Sorority having educational and professional women's pursuits. I was inducted into the Zeta Chapter of the Sorority at an Installation Banquet held at the Raleigh Hotel.[*] In connection with this affiliation among other things I undertook a study of psychology.

I also became an active member of the Business and Professional Women's Club and was involved with that organization for quite a number of years.

I was going through the dating phase of my life. I had dated in Jacksonville but nothing serious. My first date in Washington was when I had gone to the Congressional Country Club on a double date.

I dated a lawyer I had met at a Foundry Methodist Church dance who had written a book on contracts a copy of which is in the Library of Congress. This impressed me. But I'm glad I didn't marry him because I have two of the most wonderful children in the world and I couldn't have had them if I had married him. More about my marriage and children in just a little bit. The lawyer took me to Skyline Drive on a church outing and we had other dates.

I dated a fellow who took me to an overlook off the George Washington Memorial Parkway. He had ideas that didn't interest me so I asked him to take me home and he did.

Another fellow I had a date with took me to a hideaway. He also took me home when he found I wasn't interested in his pursuits. These guys!! They'll try.

---

[*] The Raleigh Hotel was later demolished. The J. Edgar Hoover FBI Building now stands on the site.

There was a fellow I had met at a party. We started dating and had a number of dates. Then there was the time that he arrived on the scene and I had a date with another fellow so we set a date to get together at another time. This time, after finding that I was dating another fellow, he came with an engagement ring.

We dated for two years. Always on Saturday nights. He didn't drive. It was always taking long walks or going to the movies. One Saturday I told him not to come for a date the next Saturday, that I planned to go with some girl friends to a Watergate Concert. He came anyway and tagged along. I think he thought I had another date. Two years after our first date we were married.

I was 25 years old when I took my marriage vows. The street-length dress I wore I had made myself. It was nothing extraordinaire.

Our marriage took place on a Wednesday in the Rectory of Our Lady of Victory Catholic Church on Conduit Road (renamed MacArthur Boulevard after World War II) where, at that time, my husband's uncle, Louis C. Vaeth, was head priest.

One couple witnessed our marriage. They were strangers to me, a couple my husband knew. I didn't know them before our marriage and I've never seen them since. I assume their names appear in some government office where there is documentation of our marriage.

There was no reception, no honeymoon. We rode the bus to Baltimore, had dinner, spent the night in The Lord Baltimore Hotel, and returned to Washington the next day.

We rented an apartment in the Alto Towers located at 3206 Wisconsin Avenue catercorner across the street from the famous Washington Cathedral.

Before my marriage, an office friend had given me a bridal shower in her home. After my marriage my Sunday School Class gave me a bridal shower. Upon my return to the office I was presented with two beautiful vanity lamps.

Back in my office in the Internal Revenue Service following my marriage. The two lamps were a wedding gift from my office. I made the dress I am wearing.

3206 Wisconsin Avenue, N.W., our first residence after our marriage. This apartment building is located catercorner across the street from the famous Washington Cathedral.

My husband, on right, talking with his uncle, Monsignor Louis C. Vaeth, who married my husband and me. This picture was taken several years after our marriage.

*Alice Vaeth*

Street cars ran from Friendship Heights where Maryland borders Washington to the downtown area of Washington. They were our method of transportation to and from our offices. At that time my husband was working the night shift at the Government Printing Office. We would wave at each other in the morning as the street car he was on traveled north on Wisconsin Avenue and the street car I was on traveled south.

Six months after we were married we left at midnight on the train to go to the World's Fair in New York City. Before we went to the fairgrounds we attended mass at St. Patrick's Cathedral. So far as I am concerned, there were two things of major interest introduced at that Fair, the television and the interstate highway system.

That night we boarded the train for our return to Washington. We had left at midnight and returned at midnight. Now, that was a very long day.

About this time I began to realize that my husband was a serious gambler. I was distressed. Money had been so precious. I had struggled because of lack of it.

During those three years between the time I had arrived in Washington and the date of my marriage I had sent a lot of money orders to my family in Jacksonville. It was so important to me to spend money wisely. To meet needs. Out of my $1,440 a year salary, I had sent about $300 in money orders each year to my family in Jacksonville. Money shouldn't be thrown away unless you're wealthy.

And, there were plans to have children. My childhood, my youth, had made me aware of the problems that can result from the lack of family planning, the disaster resulting from too many mouths to feed.

The production of children is too easy. It took man many thousands of years to develop space and other technology, yet from the beginning of time he has been able to create that which is far more awesome, another human being. Unbelievable, but we know it's true.

54

It's like, and as easy as, turning on a switch and nine months later a human being is created. God, whoever God is, may have created the first human beings but it is man who has created them since by turning on the switch with his sperm which opens the door for a baby's birth to begin.

It shouldn't be so easy to make a human being. Planning and preparation should precede the act of starting the birth of a human being. Our Creator failed to take this into consideration. He made mankind just like wild animals so far as procreation is concerned. Man is supposed to be on a higher level mentally than animals, but when it comes to sex man too often functions on the same low level mentally as animals.

There will continue to be man's idiotic turning on of the switch for a baby to be born with no exercise of his brain power. Because brain power isn't brought into play too many children are born into poverty and organizations throughout the world collect money to feed, clothe, and shelter them.

Women could exist with eggs in their uterus and never have a baby. The sperm is the switch that starts the life of a human being. Man alone has the power to control the switch. Women, of course, shouldn't make themselves available for the switch to be activated unless they are married and the family has means to care for the child properly.

Planned parenthood should be exercised by human beings. This sets the human race apart from wild animals.

Incident to my planned marriage, I had sought the advice of a doctor about birth control, so I was prepared. Our family would be planned.

Even with the best of plans and the limitation of births, we never know what lies ahead on life's road. And, so, we are always faced with fate, whatever it may be.

*Alice Vaeth*

My husband held a management position with the government but this is for naught if the income from it isn't spent wisely. His gambling would make life difficult.

Common sense dictates that if you need money for essential things you don't throw it away by gambling. And, realizing that we needed money for other things I foolishly believed that my husband would have common sense and stop gambling.

*Realistic Sense* tells us that common sense is too many times not practiced. I should have thrown up my arms and said it's not worth the agony and obtained a divorce, but I didn't and I would suffer for it later. You know: "Hope springs eternal in the human breast..." so wrote Alexander Pope.

A year after we married we moved to an apartment at 3150 16th Street next to the Mount Pleasant Library. There's a small park in front of this apartment building and it contains a statue of Marconi. Next to the apartment building on the south side is a church and farther south to the end of the block was a mulberry tree. Everyone ate those mulberries. They were delicious.

The gambling continued. It was still early in our marriage and as yet we didn't have children and none were on the way. I still expected my husband to change. Surely, I thought, if we have children he will change. Such foolish thinking. This was the time I should have left him. But I wanted so much for our marriage to work.

On a Sunday evening, coming in from one of our long walks, we turned on the radio and heard the news that the Japanese had attacked Pearl Harbor. The next day Congress declared war and World War II began.

The draft was under way. My husband was rejected because he had had meningitis of the brain as a small child and could have blackouts.

A little over 2 years after our marriage our first child was born, a son. We named him John. I marveled at this little baby lying there beside me. The wonder of it all. The experience of giving birth to another human being. The miracle of birth. My baby had little creases that looked like mother nature had just finished sewing him up. It was awesome.

One afternoon after the nurse brought my baby for me to feed him, she neglected to pick him up at the scheduled time to return him to the nursery. How wonderful, having my baby lying there beside me. I just laid there and admired this wonderful little human being I had given birth to.

We had purchased a baby crib the day before his birth. A last minute, but very important, item in preparation.

I had worked until five days before our baby's birth. World War II was raging and we were working Monday through Saturday. I had to return to work if we were to survive.

About a month after our baby's birth I returned to work. This was heartbreaking. I so much wanted to stay home and care for my baby myself. But I couldn't. We hired Dorothy Tyler to take care of our baby during the day. She was wonderful but I had so much wanted to be there myself.

Less than two years after our son was born, I was pregnant again. We hoped for a baby girl and told our less-than-two-year-old son that he would have a baby sister. He went around the apartment saying "baby sister, baby sister."

This time we had a baby girl for which we had hoped. We named her Anna Marie. We named the children after their grandparents on their father's side.

Our daughter was a beautiful baby and as awesome and wonderful as our son's birth and she was every bit as precious. Two miracles, for surely birth is a miracle. I had wanted a boy and a girl and I was

57

so fortunate to have them. They would have the companionship of each other as they grew up.

My life before I came to Washington flashed before me. I was determined that any children I had would not suffer as I had in growing up. The poverty and living conditions connected with it, especially in Florida, had not been of my making. That tent my father put in the yard in front of the house for me to live in is something better forgotten. There had been no room for me and there wouldn't be any place to take my children to. And, I had gotten away from my father and I didn't want to see him again.

With my husband's gambling there was no money for vacations anyway.

You have to live through an experience to fully understand it. Oh, if things had been different in my childhood, but they weren't.

I wanted everything to be right for my children and I would do everything I could to make it so. I must make their life a happy one.

Our baby daughter was just a little over 7 months old when word came over the radio that the Japanese had surrendered. Germany had surrendered a few months earlier, but not until the Japanese surrendered was World War II completely over.

The Atom Bomb brought about the end of the war and saved thousands of lives for the war would have gone on indefinitely without it. It actually took two Atom Bombs to end the war.

When the announcement was made that the war had ended, it was a beautiful starry night in the Nation's Capital. Happiness and celebration went into full flight.

It seemed that everyone who had a car got behind the wheel and took off for some place to celebrate. Cars, bumper to bumper, honking their horns like crazy, headed down 16th Street and probably everywhere else to celebrate. I really don't think they knew where they were going. Just on their way to some place in a spirit of hallelujah, it's over.

We were out in the little park in front of our apartment building watching, along with others, the parade of cars and listening to the continuous honking of horns. The honking was in celebration, an expression of happiness rather than for what honking is usually for. At least that's the way I interpreted it.

I was holding our seven-months-old baby daughter in my arms. My husband had our three-year-old son beside him. It was very crowded, so many people had come to the park. Suddenly I didn't see our son and I asked my husband where he was. He said some woman took him to get an ice cream cone. He didn't know who the woman was. My heart sank. He didn't know who the woman was??? How could he trust a stranger??? Where was his mind???

With my baby daughter in my arms, I rushed to the nearby drug store and there was our son seated at the counter eating ice cream with this strange lady.

This husband of mine. What should I do? What should I do? I wondered. I know everyone else has an answer but I didn't have one. It was silence and hope that things would change in the future.

Silence accomplishes nothing. But silence, coping, and hoping were so much a part of me as I tolerated problems in my growing-up years that I wasn't able to disengage myself from it. There had been no shouting and screaming at each other when I was growing up and it would not be a part of my adult life.

On Sunday we'd walk up 16th Street to Meridian Hill Park with the children. I was so proud of them, always wanting to show them off. People would exclaim what beautiful children they were.

Me with my children. Anna Marie on blanket. John sitting.

My husband holding our son John and me holding our daughter Anna Marie.

Me with our daughter Anna Marie and our son John.

Me with daughter Anna Marie on tricycle and son John standing.

I tremble all over when I think of how we took the children to the Roller Skating Rink on Kalorama Road located up a walking distance off 16th Street and I wanted everyone to admire my children. I took my baby daughter in my arms and skated around the rink. How risky! What if I had fallen? Thank God I didn't. I wanted everyone to admire my live doll.

Anna Marie with her doll

John

My daughter Anna Marie and son John on tricycle.

Me with my children Anna Marie and John.

My son John with his scooter          My daughter Anna Marie on her
                                              tricycle

My children, Anna Marie and
John.  My darlings.

One night my husband came home from work and told me he had cashed in a United States Savings Bond for money to gamble with. I knew he had cashed in insurance policies to gamble with, and now this. Some women would have said: "God damn it, I'm through with you. You've made life unlivable." But I wasn't of that temperament.

I didn't argue with him. It would have accomplished nothing. That old self-containment I had grown up with monopolized my spirit. I had grown up refraining from showing anger about problems and was so into that mind-set that my suffering was kept inside of me and not exposed.

My mind and my body function separately but in response to each other. My mind said be calm, handle it, but it was too much for my physical brain. I sat on the sofa and felt my brain going into a spin. It was like it was shaking up my mind. I was frightened, very frightened, frightened like I'd never been before in my life.

In the turmoil of my brain I worried about the children. Our son was 6 years old and our daughter was 3½-years old.

I held my head in my hands and literally forced my brain to settle down through an extremely intense mental effort. It was frightening. It was such a traumatic experience. That was a true but very difficult test of self-containment.

I was lucky to have come through that very frightening experience except for what I am about to tell you. I developed torticollis, a twisting of the neck causing the head to pull to one side. I had to hold my head in my hand to keep it facing forward. Otherwise it would twist to the left and stay there. This began an extremely difficult period.

I visited an endocrinologist who gave me injections of pituitrin and estrogen in my arm. He would inject pituitrin extract a couple times a week the first half of my menstrual cycle and would inject estrogen twice a week during the last half of my cycle. I visited the doctor's office for these injections during my lunch hour.

63

About three months after I started the injections the twisting subsided. It left me.

Unless you experience it, you can never understand how wonderful it was to get rid of the ordeal of having my head constantly turned to the left unless I held it forward.

I discontinued the injections. So wonderful to be free of the twisting. Free at last of the unbearable twisting. Right? Not so. A short time after I discontinued the injections the twisting returned so it was back to the doctor's office to resume the injections. After a short while the twisting stopped again.

This time, thinking the torticollis is likely to return as it did before, I'm afraid to discontinue the injections. So, I continued the injections for about 18 years at which time I decided to taper off my visits to the Doctor and then discontinue the visits altogether which I did and the twisting has never returned.

How much less time than 18 years it would have taken, I'll never know. It was so wonderful to be free of that horrible torticollis.

During the time I was receiving the injections, I told my husband about them hoping it would result in a cessation of his gambling. He told me he would gamble all the more if I continued to have the injections. So, I never said another word to him about the injections and had just continued to have them for 18 years.

I had gone to the bank where he borrowed money to gamble with and had begged them with tears in my eyes not to loan my husband money. The bank person I spoke with as much as laughed in my face, telling me their business was to loan money. It occurs to me that this was irresponsible banking policy. I accomplished nothing and walked away with tears still in my eyes.

My husband owed money to a fellow who lived upstairs in our apartment house. It was a gambling debt. I went upstairs and talked with the fellow and tried to get him to forget the debt. I never knew if he did or not.

Living with a gambling husband takes a lot of tolerance and that tolerance can wear thin. There is the constant struggle of trying to hold your marriage together and coping with the gambling. Only divorce would end the struggle but another struggle would ensue. His pay check did provide some funds for household needs.

I realized there was nothing I could do to change him so I wouldn't involve myself in constant arguing with him. I would have no shouting and screaming in front of the children. I would bear the burden of his gambling silently. I'm a peaceful person. Just like my mother. She had never, never, raised her voice. Neither had my older sister or others in our family.

We took the children to a restaurant for dinner. My husband ruined the evening with his carryings on. Fussing at the children about everything and nothing of any consequence. I begged him, please, can't we have an enjoyable evening. Let's put a smile on our faces, but there was no smile on his face. I was embarrassed and very hurt. I wanted so much for there to be a togetherness in our family, for us to be a happy family, but the evening was just one more time he disrupted what could have been a happy time.

Partying with friends was no fun. I avoided it. His personality was askew from acceptable conduct. My social life was practically nil during our marriage;

When the children started their schooling, I enrolled them in a Catholic school because I thought there would be more concentration on character building which to me is so very important. I'm not disparaging attendance in public schools. I, myself, did very well in public schools.

The children would grow up and could choose any religion they wished, but while they were in their formative years I wanted them to have the advantage of the morals and discipline which I felt were more greatly emphasized in Catholic schools.

Me with my daughter Anna Marie at the Queen of the May Procession

My daughter Anna Marie (front row center) in the Queen of the May Procession.

My daughter Anna Marie with the
Queen of the May.

My husband with his uncle
Monsignor Louis C. Vaeth and our
children John and Anna Marie.
John was an altar boy and is
wearing a cassock.

My wonderful children, John
and Anna Marie.

*Alice Vaeth*

The children were such a blessing. I was always so proud of them. They were so wonderful growing up.

When the children were growing up, if I became aware of a problem they were experiencing I had always stepped in to do what I could to correct it.

One morning our daughter came to me with tears in her eyes. She said she didn't want to go to school, that she was unhappy at the Catholic school she was attending. If her attendance at that school was so traumatic I didn't want her to continue there. That very morning I enrolled her in the local public school. Then I went to the Catholic school and told the Mother Superior what I had done. The Mother Superior said: "And I had thought that you were such a wonderful mother." Well, I thought to myself, my child's happiness and well-being are my foremost concern. The next year, however, she decided she wanted to return to the Catholic school and she did.

When she sold candy door-to-door for her school, I went with her and stood in the background while she rapped on doors.

I sensed that our daughter lacked self-confidence. I enrolled her in classes at a modeling school, not with the idea that she would become a model but rather that it would help her develop the self-confidence that she needed. The modeling school did help her. She developed poise and grew up to handle herself exceedingly well in any situation.

I tried so hard to keep both our son and daughter from harm. No mother has ever had two more perfect children. They never did anything wrong that was of any consequence. They were wonderful, wonderful, children. They were and are such a blessing to me. I just wish they could have had a different father. But, as we know, that is totally impossible. Their father is the only father they could ever possibly have.

When our son was just a youngster, my husband would go to his office on Saturday and, on occasion, take him along. My heart sank when my son told me later that his father had left him sitting on the front steps of the building where his father worked while his father went inside to his office.

I wanted my husband to love his children but not in that way. Our son was just a little boy at the time. Someone could have snatched him from the steps and I'd never have seen him again. I explode with emotion when 1 think of it. As a little tot his father had let him go with that strange lady to get ice cream!!!!! Nutty, nutty father, I think. It's enough to give a mother a heart attack. It almost does when I think about it.

I had absolutely no control over their father. He whipped our son when our son had done nothing to deserve it. This was grossly wrong and hurt me deeply. He was just a mean man which fact I have already established.

Throughout their childhood the children never, never, did anything to deserve being slapped or whipped. Whipping our son was unforgivable. Talking to my husband accomplished nothing.

The school held a father/son Breakfast. Our son didn't want to attend with his father because of his father's obnoxious personality. So, they didn't attend.

I doubt, in reminiscence, that their father ever loved anything other than gambling. It certainly was a love greater than for our family.

My husband's gambling and personality were almost more than I could bear. Why I coped I sometimes wonder.

Some would say I should have taken the children, slammed the door and left. Not knowing how the children would react at the time or in later years to a divorce, I decided to hold our family together.

Children can become bitter for having been deprived of one of their parents. They may go into therapy because of a divorce. It is a traumatic experience for many children who do go into therapy following a divorce.

As opposed as I am to divorce, there is one situation in which divorce should definitely take place and that is if there is child molestation, a horrible crime for which there should be the death penalty. Both fathers and mothers have been known to be child molesters. It is sad when the other parent doesn't learn about molestation until later years when it is too late to do something about it.

Raising children is an exercise in hoping and praying that everything will stay on course and that no evil will befall the family.

Life is a major undertaking that is thrust upon us when we're born. We hope we can get to the end of our life with not too many bumps in the road.

Decisions, decisions, decisions. What turn in the road to take. And, how it is impossible to return to the decision-making time and change the turn in the road.

We can't go through life without problems of one kind or another. Someone always has the answer to someone else's problems. This is wrong. No one has a right to judge someone else on personal matters. They might have done the exact same thing if they had been faced with the same circumstances.

It's important, to the extent possible, to keep adult problems from children. I never complained to the children about their father's gambling. Children should be sheltered from unpleasantness. Their life should be a happy one.

My children, John and Anna Marie, playing a game of chess.

My son, John, holding his bowling trophy

I suspect that many runaways are the result of experiencing problems in the home. It might be good to add to the marriage vows: "If we have children we will make their life a happy one."

Am I sorry I married my husband? Let's put it this way. If I hadn't married my husband, I wouldn't have my two wonderful children. They would never have existed, nor could they ever have existed for they are on this earth only because of my husband and me. There is no way they could have existed otherwise. I love them deeply. I treasure them.

While scientifically and technically man has advanced to before undreamed of heights, we are still at SQUARE 1 in human relations, i.e. too many people are. There are many decent and upright people in the world but there are far too many who have a long way to go to measure up.

I look back on my own childhood and how, in spite of anything, I never wanted my father and mother to divorce because they were the two people who had given birth to me. Absolutely no one else could have possibly done so. So, the one thing, if nothing else that I owe to my parents is my birth. Of course, there are times when I wish I hadn't been born. There was a second reason why I didn't want my parents to divorce. My mother had all those children and she never could have survived alone.

I am saddened that we could never sit down and have family discussions. Communication is so important. I wanted so much for us to be a cohesive family, to sit down around the kitchen table and work out the family budget, have family discussions, but my husband would have none of this. His sole interest was in gambling and planning and gambling don't mix.

Just as there had been no family discussions in my father's house, so now there could be no family discussions.

My husband and I could never sit and talk, chit chat. I could never carry on a conversation or have a dialogue of any length with my husband. As soon as I'd start to say something, he'd say: "Get to the point," thus shutting me up.

I gave up trying to change my husband. I had tried so hard to make things work. So, it was coping.

I took a lot of cafergot pills for recurring migraine headaches caused by the stress, and hoped that someday the children and I could find happiness.

Yes, my husband and I were truly incompatible, something I should have figured out while we were dating and something that should have set off the "don't get married" button.

If I hadn't married my husband I wouldn't have my two wonderful children. They could never have existed. Circles of thought.

I dearly love my children. They brought me the greatest happiness I ever knew or will ever know. They mean more to me than anything in the world. I wish that their childhood could have been a more happy one. I'm sure they have their own thoughts about their father and I won't attempt to read their minds for I am incapable of doing so.

When our children reached the dating age my son said: "Mother, I need a car to take my date to the Junior Prom." I think age 18 is early enough to have a driver's license. But here I was faced with the big decision and our son wasn't 18.

Buses had been our mode of transportation to and from our offices and schools and wherever else we wanted to go.

We hadn't previously owned a car. Neither my husband nor I knew how to drive. So now a car became a necessity. I bought a used Chevy for $1,000.

My daughter, Anna Marie, dating years

My son, John, dating years.

My daughter, Anna Marie, dressed for a Prom date.

Our son used the car not only for dating but also to drive his father and me to and from our offices and his sister and himself to and from school. Our offices and schools were all located within a few blocks of the U.S. Capitol Building.

Now my husband had something new to complain about. One day our son went out to the car and found the car had a flat tire. It was so ridiculous, blaming our son for the flat tire.

It's so easy to be kind and understanding so I always wondered why my husband made life so difficult for those in his own family. It occurs to me that it's in some people's blood to be mean and that they don't have the ability to change from it.

Not only does their attitude affect other's lives, they themselves must be very unhappy individuals because of their line of thinking. It's sad that there are people who function that way. Maybe if people like that got together like alcoholics do in Alcoholics Anonymous they could learn to realize how detrimental their disposition is to not only others but also to themselves.

Anyway, I now have this dating concern for soon our daughter also began to date. Now I had both children heading into an unknown future which, as a mother, I wanted so much to turn out right for them.

I kept my fingers crossed during those dating years as I assume all caring mothers do.

I could never go to sleep at night until they came home from their dates. Always looking forward to their marriage someday and wanting it to be a happy one.

Our daughter married first. Before her marriage she worked for a period in the Internal Revenue Service. Her marriage was to a fine young man, decent, clean-cut, a gentlemanly fellow. I had initially opposed the marriage because of a difference in their religions. I had always thought that my grandparents on my mother's side had

75

separated because of a difference in their religions. But, my daughter's marriage has worked out well. She did a beautiful job of converting to her husband's religion and I am very proud of her for that. She and her husband have two fine sons.

After dating a number of girls, our son met and married a beautiful very intelligent and wholesome girl who had grown up in a boarding school. If all children who go to boarding school turn out as well as this young lady did more children should go to boarding school. They had two fine children, a son and a daughter.

After several years of marriage, I was invited to my son's home for dinner, this time to tell me they were planning to get a divorce. I hated to see it happen. I had been so opposed to divorce in my own marriage. But I had to take the news and cope with it. You can't control other's lives. It's hard enough to keep one's own self from falling off the edge.

During their marriage our son had held several jobs: first as salesman, then as a Federal Government employee, and then a position in marketing with one of the largest corporations in America.

So, now our son was dating again. And, the motherly concern starts all over again.

Our son's second marriage, several years later, was again, to a very wonderful, beautiful, and very intelligent lady. They have one son.

Because of my husband's gambling, our children had experienced only apartment living while growing up. We had never been able to buy a home, it would have been mortgaged many times over to pay for gambling debts.

Now, married, each of our children own a home and each has a swimming pool. I am so happy for them.

I hope my children have a happiness that I never found in my own marriage.

Before our children's marriages my husband had begun to experience blackouts in his office where he held a management position. He told me that he would be on the telephone talking business with someone and he'd have a blackout during the telephone conversation. This, of course, had interfered with business and resulted in his retirement.

I had never witnessed my husband having a blackout but I soon would. After his retirement, he would sometimes meet me in the lobby of the Harrington Hotel, which is up the street a short distance from my office, and we'd have lunch in the hotel dining room. One day when we planned to have lunch at the Harrington and I went to the lobby of the hotel to meet him he was sitting in the lobby having a blackout. He was mumbling something during the blackout. He was completely incoherent.

After a few moments he came out of it. We had lunch. I said nothing about having witnessed the blackout but he knew I had seen it because I was there when he came out of it. He said something about it but I didn't pursue a discussion about it. I just understood.

I had known that he had had spinal meningitis of the brain as a child and had had blackouts but had always thought of it as something completely confined to his childhood.

While the children were growing up I had never witnessed him having a blackout and I really don't think he did during those years.

Whether his having had spinal meningitis of the brain had anything to do with his personality, I now wonder.

He had held a responsible management position in his office which would indicate his ability to interrelate with others in a proper manner and makes me wonder why he couldn't have had a better attitude toward his family members. But we know that this difference in attitude toward those in one's professional life and those in one's family exists.

He did, however, come home from the office one evening and made the comment: "I gave Hill hell today." Hill was the last name of someone in his office. Also, I knew he made it a practice of giving the bus driver hell. So he did spread it around.

He would fuss at me about anything. One evening I came home from work and was busy doing something, something about the apartment that had to be done. He began fussing at me. Oh, if I could only have peace, I thought.

When he was out of sight I put my jacket on, picked up my purse, walked out the door and drove the 66 miles around the Washington Beltway.

When I returned I called him from the lobby telephone to make sure he had calmed down before I went up to our apartment.

When Dr. Martin Luther King, Jr. was assassinated, I was attending a seminar in the National Archives Building at 7th Street and Constitution Avenue in downtown Washington. Archives space was being used for the seminar. The seminar had nothing to do with Archives.

About 3:00 PM we were told there was a riot going on outside and that it was taking place along 7th Street and seven blocks to the west on 14th Street.

We were told to leave the Archives Building immediately. I walked west on Constitution Avenue trying to get a cab or a bus, just any kind of transportation that would take me out of downtown Washington.

I walked fourteen blocks west on Constitution Avenue to about 21st Street before I found a bus I could board. It was jam-packed with other fleeing Government workers and I was the last one to board. I was squeezed in like a sardine but felt thankful that I had been able to get on the bus because it would soon be dark.

I was fortunate that the bus was going in my direction. I would have boarded it, however, no matter where it was going just to get out of downtown Washington.

The route the bus took was north on 16th Street which parallels 14th Street two blocks to the west. While on the bus we could see rioters coming from 14th Street with looted goods in their arms and in carts.

It wasn't until about 7:00 PM, 4 hours after I had left the Archives Building, that I arrived home about 8 miles from where I had boarded the bus.

I thought my husband would meet me at the door and say how thankful he was that I had gotten home safely. Instead, he lit into me with anger for having taken so long to get home.

I don't know what any Hell after death might be like, but I sure know what Hell on earth is like.

I just added the experience to a million others. Someday he would die and I would have peace. Or, of course, there was the possibility that I would die first and then I'd have peace. In any event, someday I would finally have peace.

Those senseless arguments. One time when he went into one of his senseless arguments I went to my son's and spent the night. My husband didn't know where I had gone. The next morning I called him to meet me up the street from our apartment for coffee. After coffee we went to our apartment.

Anything can be discussed and handled in a civilized manner, but he had his own approach to discussing matters and it wasn't in a civilized manner. Also, the things he would fuss about were of no importance. I think he had a built-in anger tank that he rolled through life with.

I was fortunate that I was in a work situation that I enjoyed. I had been promoted to the position of Personnel Clerk and went on to become Assistant Chief of the Field Management Section. In this Section we reviewed and acted on personnel recommendations emanating from the then 64 Field Collection Districts comprising a field force of approximately 30,000 employees. We also reviewed and acted on field investigative reports on field collection personnel. In addition, the Section controlled the organizational structure of the 64 Field Collection Districts.

When new administrations take over in the White House, there are always changes. When Dwight D. Eisenhower became President the work of the Collectors Organization Division of which the Field Management Section was a part was decentralized to the 64 Field Collection Districts and the Division was abolished.

Incident to the abolishment of the Division, I transferred to the Training Division of the Internal Revenue Service.

The Director of the Training Division at that time, Harold P. Zelko, was on sabbatical from Pennsylvania State University. In a letter he wrote about me, he said the following:

"She came into the Training Division during a difficult period of reorganization and worked on problems of administration, planning, budget, reporting, and general personnel matters with exceptional efficiency and ability for independent judgment.

Responsibilities included a considerable amount of writing of reports... coordinating facts, and putting thoughts into final manuscript form. I would say that she has unusual talent and ability."

Internal Revenue Service Training Division Staff in conference.
Center: Harold P. Zelko, Director of Training Division. I am second from left.

During my years as an employee of the Internal Revenue Service, I received 6 Awards from the Treasury Department and 3 Honorary Recognition Certificates from the Internal Revenue Service.

I am fourth from left, wearing corsage. Receiving a CERTIFICATE of HONORARY RECOGNITION. (I received three such awards from the Internal Revenue Service and six awards from the Treasury Department.)

The Internal Revenue Service is below the Departmental level serving as an agency within the Treasury Department.

Seeking advancement, I transferred to the Departmental level of the Post Office Department which was located across the street from the Internal Revenue Service. Here I served as Staff Assistant to the Director of the Training Division and then as Program Specialist.

I retired after serving 34 years in the Federal Government involving four different segments: first the Federal Theatre Project which was a Federal Government program, the Navy Department when I first arrived in Washington, the Internal Revenue Service, and finally the Post Office Department.

In Washington, I had been promoted from the lowly Grade 2 salary to the considerably higher level of Grade 14.

Less than 2 months after I retired from the Federal Government my husband died.

So now I was without a career and without a husband. My children were married and in their own homes. I was now alone.

When you've lived with someone for over 30 years, no matter how miserable it may have been, and how wonderful it is to be entering a period of peace, a time you have prayed for, you still face a period of adjustment. It's a matter of accepting the fact that you are now alone, and, as in my case, realizing that I always was alone in trying to keep things straight on the road of life.

The children were married and on their own. I had had them with me for too short a time. It had been so difficult. If they could be with me now things would be different, but it is too late. And I am sad. I had wanted everything to be perfect for them and it wasn't.

My husband's gambling had forced us to pinch pennies all the way through their growing-up years. His constant gambling and his difficult personality had prevented happiness in our home. If only our family life could have been different when the children were growing up. If yesterdays could be converted to more happy experiences. But they can't. They will forever be as they were.

If my married life could be relived would I do things differently? Yes, if I could have changed my husband but it's a foregone conclusion that that would have been impossible. So, I did the best I could.

If I had gotten a divorce the children would have held it against me saying I deprived them of a father. They would never understand. It's a dilemma which many mothers face.

When the children were growing up I never talked down their father to them. I didn't think it proper to do so. They could form their own opinions.

During my marriage I had put myself in a shell with my children, trying to maintain some semblance of peace in a difficult family world. Now that my husband had died I could extricate myself from

83

that shell and begin a life leaving the thorns of so many unhappy moments scattered behind me.

Now I could set about living a life of peace. I had gone through a series of so many unhappy experiences, tried to bear the brunt of those unhappy experiences and keep the children from exposure to them.

Interestingly, they blamed me for problems they had had with their father as though I should have controlled him like a ventriloquist. They blamed me for things I hadn't even known about.

I had survived my childhood with a father who beat me and gave me away to a stranger on the street, life with a husband who had made it a hell on earth for me, and now that my husband had died I was free to pursue a life of peace and happiness.

The only time in my life that I had previously had a period of peace was the approximate three years between the time of my arrival in Washington and the date of my marriage. They were three precious years. I treasure them in my memory.

# RETURN TO JACKSONVILLE AFTER 35 YEARS
## and
# SECOND CAREER AS A REALTOR®

Now that I had retired and my husband had died, I had no idea how I would spend the rest of my life. I had not given it consideration. I pondered. I tossed thoughts around in my mind. Thank goodness I still had a mind. It's a wonder that I did.

I took a course: "The Stock Market and Investment Management." I didn't own any stocks and didn't plan to invest in the stock market, but I thought it might be interesting. The stock market crash had brought on the Great Depression, so, perhaps for that reason I had a lingering interest.

Then I started to think about real estate. My father had bought and sold all those homes. My children both owned their own homes.

We had raised the children in apartments. We had continued to live in an apartment after the children's marriages. Now that my husband had died was no time for me to think about buying a home. When I had wanted a home was when the children were growing up. That's when it would have been nice to have owned a home, not when I'm going to live alone.

Real estate, that which I had never owned, sounded like an interesting subject to pursue. I'll take that back, I do own a piece of real estate. It's a cemetery lot, but I'll never live there.

So, here I am interested in real estate as a second career. I started reading books on the subject. I wanted to learn all I could about it.

I had taken many courses over the years which had facilitated my moving up the career ladder in the Federal Government. Now I'm back in class studying real estate.

I had heard that only about half of those who take the State Real Estate Examination pass it on the first try so I was elated when I passed it on the first try.

I had had a Federal Government career which had lasted over 34 years. I was now retired. So why didn't I sit back, take some exotic cruises and see the many sights I had only read about over the years?

I needed to keep busy. A workaholic. Guess I got that way from pulling all those dandelions for my father. And that's O.K. I enjoy being a workaholic. It's my nature to keep busy. Doing something.

After passing the Real Estate Examination and obtaining a Real Estate License I affiliated with one of the largest Real Estate companies in the area and went full speed ahead as an agent.

Those who make up the real estate world are widely different in their approach to pursuing the business of real estate. Those who become real estate agents enter the field from many different doors.

They may be recent college graduates, they may be second-income wives or husbands, they may be retirees from the military or civilian branches of government (such as myself), or they may be previous private industry employees, etc.

Real estate firms are understandably interested in net profit and, therefore, their interest is in a large number of ratified contracts in as high a price range as possible.

An agent, on the other hand, may be highly professional and knowledgeable, giving top notch service to the client, but may be comfortable financially without extensive real estate earnings, and, therefore, may be highly effective with clients with whom he works but may not, although they usually do, pursue volume so far as production is concerned.

The quality of an agent's services, therefore, has absolutely nothing to do with the quantity of his transactions.

The Real Estate company with which I affiliated conducted a two-week in-company training course. I took the first week of the company's two-week course and, with my sister, Loretta, who had come from her home in Michigan to visit me, got on the road in my 1969 Buick Electra for a 750 mile drive to visit the family in Jacksonville that I had left and hadn't been back to see for 35 years.

After 35 years we were still delayed one day. We spent the night in a Howard Johnson's Motel in Savannah, Georgia and expected to arrive in Jacksonville the next day. However, the next day Hurricane Agnes was playing her naughty game. In spite of the hurricane we got on the road and headed for Jacksonville, got a short distance down the road, sought shelter under an overpass, decided Hurricane Agnes was too much to battle, so I turned around and drove back to the Howard Johnson's Motel to spend another night.

The next day we arrived in the Sunshine State and there is that feeling of long ago, 35 years ago, when as a young girl I had ridden out of the State on a Greyhound Bus to go to Washington.

During those 35 years away from Jacksonville I had married, had two children each of whom had married and had two children of their own, I had retired and my husband had died.

So, here I was back where I had left 35 years before. My father had died a number of years before my return. If he had been still alive I wouldn't have returned even after 35 years away.

During those 35 years, while I hadn't been back to Jacksonville, I had seen my mother twice. Once when she was visiting her sister, my Aunt Mamie, in Mt. Morris near Flint, Michigan, I had flown there to see her. En route to Mt. Morris I stopped off in Detroit to visit my cousin Albert Roberts who was working in the Ford Motor Company. He had previously been in the military service and had come to visit me in Washington a few months after my arrival in the Nation's Capital.

Me and my cousin Albert Roberts
(Picture was taken a few months
after my arrival in Washington).

The one night I spent in Albert's home the sleeping arrangements were that I would sleep in the lower part of a bunk bed and their daughter Tracey, who normally slept there, would sleep in the upper bed. There was quite a rumpus because the daughter objected to sleeping in the top bed. I don't blame her. I wouldn't have wanted to sleep in the top bed either. We made it through the night and it was nice visiting with my cousin again and meeting his lovely family that I hadn't met before.

The next day it was back on the plane and to Mt. Morris to see my mother at my Aunt Mamie and Uncle George's home.

Needless to say, we had a wonderful visit. I spent several days there before returning to Washington and to my office in the Internal Revenue Service.

The airplane in which I flew from Detroit to Flint, Michigan

Left to right: Aunt Mamie Lowell, me, my mother, my sister Loretta

The second time I had seen my mother during those 35 years was when she was 75 years old and I had sent her money for a plane ticket to Washington. I had also included money for a plane ticket to Washington for my sister Mary because of a trip I planned to take with them after their arrival in Washington.

It was so wonderful to see my mother again. It was about six years since I had seen her at my Aunt Mamie's in Mt. Morris and about two years before I would make the trip back to Jacksonville.

My mother wasn't aware of all the problems I had with my husband and I didn't ruin her visit by getting into a discussion of them. Everyone has their own problems, whatever they may be. It was my practice to keep my problems to myself. I had always done that. That old self-containment was so much a part of me.

My mother and my husband had a few laughs over what they read or have read in the funny papers. They were both avid readers of the funny papers. I had never taken time to read the funny papers so I couldn't share in their laughs.

The whole idea of my inviting my mother and my sister to Washington was not only because my mother had reached her 75th birthday but also because I wanted for us to drive to Muncie, Indiana where I had started school in the first grade and where my sister Mary was born.

With my mother and my sister Mary I drove to my sister Loretta's home in Adrian, Michigan. We spent the night with Loretta and early the next morning the four of us got in my Buick for a one-day trip to Muncie. On the road we stopped in a wayside inn for breakfast, drove west to Interstate 69 and south to Muncie, the place we had left so many years before.

Left to right: My sister Mary Ellis, my mother Grace Lacey, and me ready to leave for Adrian, Michigan, to pick up my sister Loretta and drive to Muncie, Indiana, the place of my sister Mary's birth.

My sister, Loretta Montgomery

Me by my 1969 Buick Electra in front of my sister Loretta's home in Adrian, Michigan

We had lunch in Muncie. We then drove to the Roosevelt Elementary School to take a picture of the school. I thought about my teacher, Miss Frye, who had given me that pretty little dress and matching panties having felt sorry for me because of the rags I wore. I thought that if she were living now I would invite her to Washington and take her to the Kennedy Center. And, all those other people who had been so wonderful to me when I was growing up. I'd invite them all to Washington and I'd throw a big party at one of the city's swankiest restaurants. It's too late. They are gone. Life goes on and I have to travel along with it. But my heart is full of love for those wonderful people who befriended me in my childhood.

After taking a picture of the Roosevelt School we drove to the home my father had built and where we had lived so many years ago. We asked the family living in the house if they would let us see the inside. They did and inside we began pointing things out about my father's architecture, the rooms we remembered, how my mother had given birth to my sister Mary while we were living in that house, how my sister Loretta and I had walked out the door early in the morning

91

to go to the dairy to get milk, how I had been outside, walked in a mud puddle, had ruined my shoes, and could never wear them again, how my sister, Loretta, and I would leave the house and walk up the street to go to school.

Those beautiful flower beds that were part of my father's landscaping were long gone. But the house still stood and that was interesting.

I thought about having left Muncie and riding the train to Ft. Smith, Arkansas, and all that followed.

You hear about memories that bless and burn. That's exactly what those memories did. It was nostalgic.

That evening we returned to my sister's home in Adrian. On our return trip I made it a special point to stop for dinner at the same wayside inn where we had stopped for breakfast that morning. On our trip to Muncie it suddenly hit me that we had left the inn that morning without my paying for our breakfast and I was anxious to get back there and pay them. So, we had dinner and I paid for both breakfast and dinner. I'll never understand how that happened but strange things happen and that was one of them. I'm a stickler for honesty.

The next day, after spending the night with my sister Loretta, we got on the Interstate and headed back to Washington.

Those Interstates, so much a part of our world today, didn't exist when I was a young girl. The Federal Aid Highway Act signed June 29, 1956 inaugurated the interstate highway system.

Now, I never knowingly or intentionally exceed the speed limit. My eyes are always on the road. Looking at the speedometer takes my eyes off the road. So I keep up with the traffic and now and then pass other cars.

Almost home, I'm on the Washington Beltway and I'm stopped by a highway patrolman. He said I was exceeding the speed limit and when I told him I was driving at the same speed as the other cars he said I was passing cars. He gave me a ticket. That was the finale to our trip to Muncie. It was a wonderful trip.

A few days later I drove my mother and my sister Mary to the airport for their return to Jacksonville.

It was two years later that I drove with my sister, Loretta, to Jacksonville after my 35 years away.

What a trip that was, returning after 35 years. It was getting acquainted with your own family. The two sets of twins that had been born to my mother after my high school graduation and were babies when I had left Jacksonville to go to Washington were grown, married, and had children of their own.

The area had flourished during those 35 years. Businesses had appeared on the scene and the population had grown significantly. Country roads had become city streets.

My mother, now a widow, was living with my bachelor brother Clarence Arthur Lacey who had served in World War II, had returned from the war, and had bought the home he and my mother were living in. After my father died my mother had sold the home I had known.

My brother Clarence Arthur Lacey with our mother Grace Lacey.

My brother, Clarence Arthur Lacey. He served in the Air Force in World War II.

There was a cake and celebration. 35 years is a long time, a very long time, a life time for some people. There were a lot of hugs and kisses. A reunion long overdue.

"Welcome Home Sisters" cake when I returned to Jacksonville after having been away for 35 years. During those 35 years I had married, had two children who had grown up and gotten married, and each had two children of their own. I had retired after almost 35 years in the Federal Government and my husband had died.

The next day after arrival, my sister Loretta Montgomery who had made the trip to Jacksonville with me, my sister Lucille Lightbourn and my mother and I got in my Buick for a 1,000 mile trip to San Antonio, Texas to visit my brother Leroy who had been about 5 years old when I had last seen him at the time I had left Jacksonville to go to Washington.[*]

Leroy had served in the Korean War following which he worked in the civilian branch of the Federal Government.

---

[*] I mentioned earlier in this book that my mother was pregnant when we moved from Adrian, Michigan to Jacksonville. Leroy is the one she was pregnant with.

We enjoyed so much visiting with Leroy, his wife Rita, and their children in their comfortable suburban home. We took advantage of the trip to visit the Alamo.

Left to right: My brother Leroy Lacey, my sister Lucille Lightbourn, my mother, me, and my sister Loretta Montgomery.

My brother Leroy Lacey with his wife, Rita, and three sons Ricky, Gary, and Randy.

We spent two nights in motels driving to San Antonio and two nights in motels returning to Jacksonville.

There are a couple things I'll mention about our drive to and from San Antonio. On the way to San Antonio traveling west, as you approach the New Orleans area, Interstate 10 takes you south and through the downtown section of the city instead of continuing directly west on the northside of the city. I think it was poor planning to have the Interstate dip down into the business section of New Orleans instead of continuing directly west. Maybe the highway planners did this to bring traffic into the center of the city for business. I don't know but I think it was poor planning.

Driving through the downtown section it was bumper to bumper. Ambulances were trying to squeeze through the traffic and I was suffering from an unbearable headache. It would have been nice to have had lunch in New Orleans but with that traffic I just wanted to get out of there. If I ever drive through that area again and I want to bypass New Orleans I'll continue west on the road which runs east and west on the north side of New Orleans, the stretch of road that should be Interstate 10 instead of some other number which has been assigned to it.

The other thing I want to mention about that trip is that on our return trip to Jacksonville, as we were driving east, water from Mobile Bay splashed up onto my car windshield. Now, I've never before experienced water splashing on my windshield from a waterway. The people who live in that area probably experience that all the time but to me it was a novel experience.

On that trip to and from San Antonio and those nights in motels we had a lot to talk about and there was a wonderful togetherness. We did a lot of reminiscing.

Left to right: Me, mother Grace Lacey, sister Loretta Montgomery, and sister Lucille Lightbourn at a motel en route to San Antonio

Left to right: My mother Grace Lacey, me, and my sister Lucille Lightbourn. The Gulf of Mexico is in the background.

Left to right: My sister Loretta Montgomery, my sister Lucille Lightbourn, and me.

After our return to Jacksonville we continued our family togetherness. We did a lot more reminiscing and a week later my sister, Loretta, and I returned to Washington and Loretta returned to her home in Michigan.

So now I'm back in Washington in my apartment and alone. My husband had died a year before I had made the trip back to Jacksonville.

When I had left Jacksonville 35 years earlier I had come to Washington to begin a career in the Federal Government which lasted 34 years. Now my trip from Jacksonville to Washington was to begin my second career, this time as a Real Estate Agent. I decided I would spend 25 years in this second career.

I delved into my new career as a Real Estate Agent. I took the second week of the company's two-week training course. This training dealt primarily with rules, regulations, and laws relating to real estate.

The classes were held in downtown Alexandria, Virginia. It's a historical area which added pleasure to drive across the Potomac river to attend the classes.

It was only three years before I became a real estate agent that I bought my first car, the 1969 Buick Electra that I made the trips to Muncie, Jacksonville, and San Antonio in. I bought that car the week the Astronauts landed on the moon. A car is an absolute necessity in real estate. All those years working in downtown Washington in the Federal Triangle I had always ridden streetcars or buses. I had had no desire to own a car. (The car I had bought previously was for my son when he was dating. It was always his car.)

After I had taken lessons and learned to drive I hadn't immediately bought a car. I had rented cars for about a year. While driving one of those rented cars, I was stopped by a highway patrolman. He said the sticker on the car had expired and was going to give me a ticket until I explained that it was a rented Hertz car.

Another newly licensed agent who had attended the company training at the same time I did, and I, sequestered ourselves in a conference room for a week to study all the various types of transactions and the forms and procedures relating to each so that we could conduct ourselves professionally and not fumble with the details in working with clients. Actually, we studied what you might call the nuts and bolts of putting a real estate transaction together which had not been covered fully in the formal training.

Just as I had started with a goal and an inward push to succeed in my Federal Government career, now I did the same thing in my Real Estate career. I exercised the same zeal as I had in my Federal Government career. I was young at heart.

I went full speed ahead getting listings and making sales. I pursued real estate designations by documenting millions of dollars in Real Estate settlements and taking additional courses to obtain the GRI (GRADUATE of the REALTORS INSTITUTE) and even more courses to obtain the CRS (CERTIFIED RESIDENTIAL SPECIALIST) designation. Having obtained the designations I could include them on my business cards.

All real estate agents in the Washington area are required to continue their real estate education following licensing. A specified number of educational credits in each of specified calendar periods is required in order to retain a real estate license.

I was licensed as a real estate agent in Washington, D.C., Maryland, and Virginia, so I had to acquire follow-up educational credits required in each of these jurisdictions.

I had never dreamed as a raggedy hungry little kid that someday I'd be listing and selling homes in the Nation's Capital, Washington, D.C. And, not only in Washington, but also in the surrounding areas of Maryland and Virginia.

And, that I'd be sitting in lawyers' offices at conference room tables participating in real estate settlements for doctors, military officers, government officials, television personalities and even a Nobel Prize winner (Dr. Frederick C. Robbins – Physiology/Medicine 1954 Won Nobel Prize together with Dr. John F. Enders and Thomas H. Weller for their discovery of the ability of poliomyelitis viruses to grow in cultures of various types of tissue.) as well as many wonderful people of all economic and educational levels from all over the United States and the world (Canada, South Africa, Nigeria, United Arab Republic, Singapore, Thailand, Japan, England, Norway, and others).

Settlements are the finale of buying or selling a home. Many hours and much ground is covered in arriving at the point of settlement on a home. An instructor told us that settlement must be like coming in for a smooth landing at the airport. In other words, no wrinkles at the settlement table.

Here I was listing and selling homes and I'd never owned a home of my own. Buyers and sellers I worked with, if they happened to find out that I list and sell real estate and don't myself own a home would sometimes question why. They would have to know the story of my life to understand. I always changed the subject as gracefully as possible.

There were many exciting and some not so pleasant experiences in real estate. Like the time I removed the key from the lockbox and opened the door of the home to show it to a prospective buyer. The burglar alarm went off. With my prospective buyer beside me, I went to a neighbor's home on the cul de sac and called the listing agent relating what had happened. She called the owner who was away on vacation to get the code to turn the alarm off. She got the code, called me back and gave it to me. I returned to the home with my prospective buyer, turned the alarm off and proceeded to show the home. Then the doorbell rang. I opened the door. There stood a policeman, gun in hand. I proceeded to explain what had happened. I could hardly keep from laughing. It was really funny seeing a policeman standing there with a gun in his hand when I was just trying to show a house. If you see me walking down the street with a smile on my face it could just be because that incident flashed across my mind.

When I finished explaining what had happened, the policeman put his gun in its holster. The other policemen who surrounded the home all came to the front of the home and they drove away in their cars.

The owner of the home and the agent who listed the home for sale should, of course, have done whatever was necessary so that agents showing the home would not be faced with that kind of experience.

Agents write sale contracts reflecting the offering price of the prospective purchaser. The offering price is many times below the price at which the home was listed for sale.

No matter how low the offer is, the agent must present the contract offer to the seller. Only the seller has the right to decline or ratify a contract offer. Of course, agents try to write full-price contracts, but they don't refuse to write low offers.

Sometimes an agent, knowing that another offer or offers are going to be presented at a particular time, will advise the buyer for whom he or she is going to present an offer, and the buyer will raise the price of his offer up to or above the price at which the home was listed in order to have a better chance of having his contract offer ratified. This is not an unusual occurrence.

I always tried to write full-price offers. However, I was at a contract presentation where the offer I had brought for the listing agent to present contained a low offering price. The listing agent explained to the sellers that the home had been on the market for some time, that his office had discussed the need to lower the asking price, and he urged the sellers to ratify the contract offer which I had brought to the table. The wife called her husband who was away on a trip and they together decided to ratify the contract I had brought. The lady had pen in hand, started to write her signature on the contract when the telephone rang. It was another agent who had a contract to present. At that moment everything stopped dead cold. We sat and waited for the agent to arrive with his contract. He did and his contract, containing a higher dollar figure, was ratified.

I listed a home in the very popular area of Foggy Bottom in downtown Washington. I had six contracts, written by six different agents, to present to the owner at one sitting. That's an agent's dream.

I listed a home in beautiful Flower Valley in suburban Maryland that caused me great anguish. The home was going to foreclosure. I found the family a rental home several miles south of the Washington Beltway where they could live while I tried to find a buyer for their home.

Another agent wrote a contract for a prospective buyer and gave me the contract to present to the sellers since I was the listing agent.

Accompanied by an agent friend, I drove down Interstate 95 south of the Washington Beltway to Dale City, Virginia where I had rented the sellers a home to present the contract.

As is customary, before going through the terms of the contract, I showed the sellers the deposit check and the Financial Information Sheet reflecting the prospective buyer's ability to purchase the home.

Then I started to go through the terms of the prospective buyer's contract offer.

When I mentioned the low offering price, the wife became irate. She walked to the kitchen, picked up a butcher knife, walked back into the living room where I was presenting the contract, and, pointing the butcher knife at me, said: "You get out of my house."

I was afraid to run for fear she'd run after me. So I walked to the door and out. I was really frightened. I stood by my car shaking.

The agent who had accompanied me to the contract presentation had been a Foreign Service Officer before becoming a real estate agent. When I walked out of the home, he continued to sit in the living room and kept his cool. After all, he wasn't the one she threatened. It was me because I was their agent and was, therefore, the one who was presenting the contract. I'm convinced that my agent-friend's previous experience in the Foreign Service helped him to keep his cool. A couple minutes later he joined me and we drove back to our office.

Agents are required to present all contract offers regardless of the offering price, and sellers need to understand this. Agents should make this clear to sellers at the time of listing a home for sale and it would be well to reiterate it when presenting a low price offer. Only the seller has the right to reject or ratify an offer.

Another agent asked me to work with her in listing and selling a home on Constitution Avenue about two blocks east of the U.S. Capitol Building.

A sweet little well-dressed and immaculate lady who sold cosmetics door-to-door was renting the home. The home was filthy. She had cats in different rooms and had screen doors to the rooms so the cats couldn't mix and mingle. The home was so filthy that whenever I went there I wore a scarf over my head and the rest of my clothing would be something that I could take off and wash as soon as I got home. Then, of course, I'd take a bath. I'll never understand how the lady who was renting the home could be so immaculate and live in that filth.

This wasn't the only home I found filthy in my real estate career. Among others, it was shocking to find a number of doctors' homes that way, but this wasn't typical of doctors' homes.

When there's a filthy home and a divorce is taking place you wonder if the husband could no longer stand the filth. And, when there is a filthy home and no divorce is taking place you can't help but think that they each found their equal.

Real estate work can be hazardous. It is fraught with many dangers. A Virginia real estate agent who didn't have a Washington real estate license referred to me a client who owned a home which the owner's deceased husband had purchased as an investment. The home is located on Hanover Place off North Capitol Street a few blocks north of the U.S. Capitol Building.

It isn't a good idea to turn down referrals because doing so could cut off future referrals. And, referrals are an important adjunct to other real estate pursuits.

So, I listed the home, put it on the market, and showed it to a number of prospective buyers. And, I wrote a contract offer for a prospective purchaser which was ratified by the owner.

When I had listed the home for sale I had had an uncomfortable feeling about the neighborhood but had no knowledge of the serious drug problem that was later reported by The Washington Post Staff Writer Linda Wheeler to have existed on that one-block-long Hanover Place.[*] As much as I appreciated referrals, I would never have gone into that neighborhood and listed that home had I been aware of the drug market on that one-block street.

_____

[*] The Washington Post, December 14, 1989.

103

Real estate is a 24-hour-a-day job. Well, not quite, but almost. I had a contract to present to a doctor who was on night duty at an Alexandria, Virginia hospital. At 2:00 AM in the morning, I presented the contract to the doctor in the hospital.

It isn't smart to wait to present a contract because another agent could register a contract and it could be ratified and you'd lose a sale. So, regardless of the time of day, you present a contract as soon as possible. I wouldn't, of course, wake someone up to present a contract.

In another case, an agent called me at 9:00 o'clock at night to register a contract on one of my listings, and, of course, he wanted it presented that night. As the listing agent it was my responsibility to present the contract to the sellers. Hurriedly I got out of my pajamas, into my street clothes, and I was off to the home of the sellers a quarter way around the Washington Beltway to present the contract.

There are so many, many, more stories I could relate. Real estate is exciting. So many wonderful and not-so-wonderful experiences.

Buyers and sellers have no idea of the amount of work involved in an agent's earning his or her commission. There is an immense amount of work involved from the time of first buyer or seller contact and the time of settlement, and oftentimes beyond.

Now and then there is a quickie, but these are needed to offset in part the work involved in most transactions.

Not only did I find working with buyers and sellers a wonderful experience, but I found the majority of real estate agents to be wonderful colleagues.

Years ago when I had retired from a 34-year career in the Federal Government, had made the trip to Jacksonville after having been away for 35 years, then had made my second trip to Washington to pursue a real estate career, I had planned to spend 25 years as a real estate agent.

With my 25 years as a real estate agent completed, I turned in my real estate licenses and began to look for other fields of interest.

*Alice Vaeth*

# CONCERNS

Having retired from my second career, that of Real Estate Agent, I became more interested in issues of the day, things that weighed on my mind and which concerned me, things which I thought something should be done about. I'd write letters expressing my view and I'd engage friends in a discussion of events. Workaholic Alice had to stay involved, if not with a particular profession then with life itself.

Retirement is a time to sit back and explore life and the world around you in a way that you never found time for before. It's an in-depth look at what was only surface thinking before. My concerns extend into many issues. I'll discuss a few of them.

First, today's children. They are different than yesterday's children. The avalanche of violence and sex on television is a major reason. "Monkey see, monkey do" is exactly what's happening. Too many children are seeing and doing. As a result many become criminals.

If our forefathers had had a crystal ball I believe they would have written the 1st Amendment to the U.S. Constitution differently as regards free speech. Our forefathers knew nothing about television and all those other current sources of evil thought.

Freedom is great. That's what America is all about. We love America for that reason. We must admit, however, that freedom has limits. For instance, we don't have freedom to do harm to other people. There is no freedom there. If we do harm to other people we can end up in a court of law. Too many do.

This thing about not having the freedom to do harm to other people should apply to the producers of evil who do harm to other people who happen to be little children. Many children commit crime and end up in prison because of their evil learnings from products of those producers.

*Alice Vaeth*

So many, many, stories could be told about what has happened as a result of children watching evil productions. They watch a movie and go out and commit horrible crimes because of what they have seen in the movie.

The television isn't something that is kept under lock and key. It's as available to children as is the refrigerator door and the kitchen table. We wouldn't feed harmful food to our children and we shouldn't let them be harmed by the television set. The television is a teacher of how to commit crime. What kind of a civilization are we pursuing?

We need legal action to place restrictions on producers. Otherwise, we cannot expect them to change the contents of their outputs. They are teaching little children how to perform evil acts. They are a detriment to civilization.

Changing for the sake of keeping little children from a life of crime would cause the producers of evil to lose vast fortunes. Evil is a money maker, a fortune maker. A line should be drawn somewhere to protect our children. And, I might add, to not put ideas in the minds of evil adults.

No political campaign funds should be accepted from producers of films, videos, and such.

Protecting our children. It's a great responsibility. We can't put our children in our pocket and carry them around with us 24 hours a day. They are with a nanny, in nursery school, in regular school, in Boy Scout or Girl Scout meetings, and other places where parents are not with them. Since we don't always know what those outside influences might consist of, it's a matter of providing parental guidance as to: "If some particular thing should happen, you should…"

Parental guidance throughout childhood and the adolescent years in all avenues of a child's life is crucial to a child's proper development.

Something happens many times during the away-from-parent time that affects the child adversely and could be the seed of disaster, but the child does not tell a parent. Subsequently a parent learns about it after it has developed into partial or total disaster.

To guard against this, every family should sit down together around the table in the dining room or kitchen, or comfortably in the family room, or wherever, every evening and discuss what happened in each of their lives during the day.

Because of conflicting schedules of family members, it may not be possible for all family members to always be present, but such meetings, perhaps called "family get togethers," should be held on a regular basis with all available family members present.

Hopefully such family get togethers would bring to the surface any problems in the bud at a time when something could be done about the problem. Uncovering all problems may not be possible because a child may choose to cover up for a guilty one. But, the effort should be made to uncover all problems so they can be dealt with.

Love and caring within the family can be a great magnet for a child. Every child wants to be loved and cared about and the family get-togethers would be evidence of that love.

I regret that there were no such meetings in my father's house or in raising my own children but I hope my children and my grandchildren realize the benefits of family get-togethers.

Hugs and kisses at appropriate times are so important. They weren't part of my growing-up years. I didn't realize the importance of them until my children were grown and married. I regret this. I was always alert to anything I needed to do to protect my children but I realize now that I neglected the hugs and kisses and I am sorry for that.

*Alice Vaeth*

I am concerned about our schools and how they affect our children who go in and out of their doors. It is not enough to teach children reading, writing, arithmetic and those other scholastic subjects. Schools must be concerned about much more than that.

Many children in our schools today will some day become criminals. We know this to be a fact. To overlook this reality is to put blinders on our eyes. Our efforts must be to stop the drift of so many children into criminal activity. This must be the focus of our schools.

The Supreme Court ruled on June 17, 1963 that laws requiring recitation of the Lord's Prayer or Bible verses in public schools are unconstitutional. This is as it should be. Let places of worship take care of religion.

A Code of Ethics is more appropriate for schools. Including appropriate utterances in a school Code of Ethics would do much to center a child's mind on what it means to be a good member of society. Our schools should concentrate on good citizenship and decency.

Following is a suggested Code of Ethics:

### CODE of ETHICS
### for Students

I will obey all laws.
I will respect proper authority.
I will have self-respect.
I will respect the rights of others.
I will solve any problems I have in a proper manner.
I will be honest, trustworthy, and charitable.
I will exercise self-control.
I will handle disappointments with dignity.
I will be kind to others.
I will not be swayed by evil forces.

It would be well for each student to write down for the teacher what each line of the Code of Ethics means to him. This would help the student to understand how he should apply what he speaks in the Code of Ethics. There could be a class discussion about the meaning of each line of the Code of Ethics.

The teacher should provide guidance to problem students where necessary in a way that doesn't reflect negatively on the student, and is not embarrassing to the student (privately, not in front of other children).

Children like friends just as all human beings do and the teacher as a friend can accomplish a lot. The teacher should consider her role as not only one of pouring out book knowledge but also one of character building.

If the teacher shows kindness and understanding she has an opportunity to turn the recalcitrant child around. The teacher needs to establish herself as a caring person when she first stands before a class.

Teachers have an awesome responsibility. They serve in an arena of minds from all segments of our society, minds which do not always blend comfortably together in the classroom. A wise teacher will be able to handle diversity well.

A good teacher, one who is fully committed and understands the calling of her profession, puts the mind of the student in good working order.

Some of our teachers, I believe, do not know what excellence in teaching is all about. They put in 8 AM to 4 PM time, or whatever their hours are in the classroom, go home and grade papers, and feel they have fulfilled their responsibility. They go home at night and say to themselves: "I'm glad to be away from those brats."

They lack the caring and sensitivity to a child's character needs and therein, I believe, lies a big part of the problem in our schools today, especially as there is disrespect for the teacher.

Teachers fill a role that is of a much higher calling than most other professions because they mold the minds of children for life.

Many a great and prosperous man as an adult has praised a teacher who taught him in his youth. The teacher who molds the mind with excellence is a great treasure.

Excellence in teaching should be rewarded with a gold medal.

Kindergarten, the place where children start growing up beyond babyhood and tothood, is the place to start teaching children what it means to be a good person, a future good citizen, for this is as important in their development as learning how to read and write, etc.

Beginning in kindergarten everything children learn is put on a mental shelf for later retrieval. A lot of good seeds can be planted in their minds at this early age.

For example, by playing out the story of the old woman who lived in a shoe and had so many children she didn't know what to do children can learn the importance of having both a mother and father in the home, that if something happens to the father and the mother is left to care for the children alone the mother may become destitute and need assistance, and that people should help her. This would teach children kindness.

Many lessons can be taught from nursery rhymes and children's stories should be used for this purpose.

In the first or second grade authority should be explained to students. They should be told that authority is in place to keep things running smoothly, that without authority there would be chaos. If they understand the reason for authority they will appreciate it.

The teacher's role and the policeman's role should especially be explained. They should be told that the teacher and the policeman are interested in their well-being. If it is explained to them properly they will respond with appreciation for authority.

It would be well to invite a policeman into the classroom and let the children shake his hand and exchange pleasantries.

Many problems in the school, on the playground, and elsewhere result from a lack of basic manners. Too many children don't know how to interrelate in a civilized manner. They become the problem children in our schools and in our communities.

Too many children enter school without having learned the importance of such simple utterances as "Thank you," "I'm sorry," "Would you please?" "Could I help you?," etc.

As a result many arguments and disagreements result in fights and sometimes there are tragic consequences. Children need to understand the benefits of good behavior, how it enhances their image and success in life. Since so many children don't learn the above utterances at home, they should be taught them in school.

Discipline should be at the top of the chart for grading purposes throughout school. It reflects stability and character and is such an extremely important part of the learning process. It has a lot to do with the future success of the student.

All because of a lack of discipline, many children get on the wrong track, get lost, and can't find their way back. They find themselves in prison with a revolving door through which they leave with thoughts on rails that have no good end.

It's important for children to understand how discipline can benefit them personally, that it isn't just a matter of conforming. They should be told that good character enhances their potential for success and happiness in life.

Discipline is enhanced by the child learning decency, charity, honesty, respect for authority, self-control, and much more.

Starting in kindergarten, through the upper grades, as well as through the higher learning years, discipline should be emphasized. It is of major importance throughout life's journey.

In Home Economics class children are taught that they need a proper balance of protein, carbohydrates, fat, vitamins, minerals, water, and roughage to help their body grow and replenish itself properly.

In the same class they should be taught that certain things, if they enter the body, can interfere with the proper functioning of their mind and body, that they only have one mind and body to last them a lifetime, that their mind and body are precious and they need to take good care of them.

They should be told that there are people who will try to sell them harmful drugs on the street even though it is against the law to sell such drugs. They should understand that such drugs can play havoc with their mind, that it is most important that they always have control of their own mind and not use drugs.

Similarly, they should be taught that alcohol can make them lose control of their mind and, therefore, they shouldn't drink alcohol. At least not to excess. Maybe a glass of wine. Not at all is best.

As for tobacco, they should be shown a stovepipe filled with black soot and it should be explained to them that tobacco can create soot in their lungs, that in many cases soot in the lungs causes early death.

Emphasis should be put on keeping a healthy mind and body because what they have are the mind and body they can expect to last a lifetime.

Schools are all about preparing students for adulthood and employment is a very important part of adulthood. Thus it is important that students have employment capability when they end their formal education at whatever level that may be.

Classes should be available in subjects that relate directly to work aspirations and opportunities.

Our criminal justice system has programs to prepare inmates and parolees for employment. The mission of our schools should be to prepare students for employment and then maybe many of them wouldn't become inmates or parolees.

Suspending children from school, putting them out to roam the streets, provides a door for them to enter the world of crime if they're not already a part of that world. It is detrimental to both them and the community. The street is definitely not where they should be.

Every day in school is valuable because of the lessons learned, lessons they'll go through life without if they are roaming the streets instead of being in class.

There should be some other form of punishment and it must be something that he will fear, otherwise it accomplishes nothing. Let me emphasize, it must be something he will fear.

There are scheduled vacation times for the student body. Children's interest in out-of-school activities should be explored by a check-off sheet two or three months before the summer and other out-of-school periods begin.

Out-of-school activities are very important in the extended development of children beyond the school grounds. Such activities can play an important role in the child's development.

There can and should be neighborhood, community, and other organized activities of sufficiently interesting character to keep children involved in worthwhile activities during those out-of-school times.

Some children are interested in sports activities, some in library reading perhaps with book reporting in a group situation with one's peers. Some may be interested in the culinary arts, some may be interested in volunteer work perhaps mentoring other students who need help in their studies, some in arts and crafts, some in farming, forestry, or ranching, some in animal care, etc. Some may have a combination of interests.

Whatever their interests, they should be explored and programs planned.

When out of school, it is also a wonderful time for children to visit museums and other points of interest. Of course, some children will be going on vacation with their families.

These vacation-time activities don't have to be costly. They shouldn't require an Act of Congress to implement them. Citizens interested in their community should develop and conduct programs based on feedback from questionnaires filled out by students.

Such programs can be sponsored by community organizations, by parents, by religious organizations without religion input unless the program is only for members of the particular religious group, or by corporate or other company planning.

Such activities could be very helpful in keeping children on the right track.

There is a concern about how children handle sex when they learn about it. The fact that there is such a thing as sex, I believe, children in the past first learned about it from a peer. In today's world most children probably learn about it from watching television.

I personally learned about sex when I was about nine years old. Walking home from school, a classmate explained to me how babies are born. Now, to me and my classmates babies are born only to mothers and fathers who are married. That meant that only at such time as I would be married would I have anything to do with sex and having a baby.

The fact that you shouldn't have sex before you are married was imprinted on my mind by classmates pointing to a particular house and saying: "That's where the girl lives who had sex and she wasn't married." She was scorned.

America has changed and it's now more difficult for children to have high morals. I hope that the majority of them do, but too many of them don't. They have allowed themselves to drift with the tide of sex without marriage. This is called "cheap." It's giving one's body away without being married. It's reducing one's self to an animal of the wild.

In the last half of the 20th century loose sex gained a footing in western Europe then spread across the ocean to America. And, women's lib came into prominence.

Love became disengaged from sex in an increasing number of relationships. We began to hear this thing about partners and having sex with multiple others.

I say love became disengaged. Well, it is probably there to some degree but in a different kind of way than in a stable marriage relationship.

Sex has mounted the throne as a primary consideration for a relationship in too many cases. How wild!! People have reverted to animal-type relationships. It's sickening.

Women should realize that they are on a higher plateau in life than animals, that there should be a difference between humans and beasts in sexual activity.

Women's lib has led us in the wrong direction. It has reversed civilization. It has cheapened women. We need to take a turnaround and restore respectability to women.

Appropriate women's organizations should take the lead and send representatives to high school classrooms to speak to students about how sex should be properly handled. This would be a noble cause for women's organizations to pursue.

They should explain to students that they are above the animal world, that people should have sex only if they are married. Also, students should be told that when they marry uppermost in their mind should be that they should only have children if they love children and have the means to care for them.

Only women have the door for babies to be born and enter this world. Men do not have that door. The door is controlled by women. So, women are in the driver's seat so far as pregnancies are concerned. They control the door to begin a pregnancy. They can open or close that door, and they should open it only if they are married.

Students should understand the importance of compatibility in a marriage. This should be stressed. It is so important if the marriage is to be a happy one.

Incompatibility is a major reason for divorce. According to the U.S. National Center for Health Statistics, Vital Statistics of the United States, in 1998 there were approximately 2,244,000 marriages and approximately 1,135,000 divorces in the United States. In other words, approximately half of all marriages in the United States end in divorce. Students should look at these figures and realize the importance of exploring compatibility before marriage. They should keep in mind that a child deserves both a mother and father and that if a divorce happens a child would have only one to live with.

It should be impressed on girl students that incident to their planning a wedding date they should obtain knowledge of ways to avoid unwanted or unaffordable pregnancies. They may wish to consult a physician, as I did, about birth control. This would hopefully prevent a lot of abortions.

Concurrently with discussing planned parenthood with students, women's organizations should pursue ways to handle the abortion problem which will no doubt continue to exist regardless of the lecturing to students.

It's a paradox. While protestors seek life for the unborn child, they injure and kill pro-abortionists.

If the mother-to-be doesn't want the child, what kind of care could we expect the mother to give the child if it lives? A child should be wanted and loved when it comes into the world.

If the protestor really loves the unborn and wants it to live, the protestor should logically also want the child to have proper care after it is born.

Accordingly, women's organizations should pursue bringing about the following which would require protestors to link their protesting to certain action on their part:

1.    Protestor agrees to sign legal papers prepared by an attorney and by a prospective mother specifying that the protestor agrees to adopt the mother's baby when it is born even though the child may be deformed or have some physical or mental curable or incurable disease.

OR

2.    Protestor agrees to place the baby in an orphanage which the protestor would be instrumental in setting up for children who would otherwise be aborted. (NOTE: Many children raised in orphanages have grown up to do better in life than others living in a home with a mother and father. Read: "The Home: A Memoir of Growing up in an Orphanage" by Richard McKenzie, Professor at the School of Management, University of

119

California at Irvine, who is an alumnus of the Barium Springs Home for Children in North Carolina.)

OR

3.     Protestor sets up an Adoption Agency specifically for children who would otherwise be aborted.

OR

4.     Protestor raises money for poor women to care for unplanned children if they seek abortion.

Any of the above would be a positive and commendable way for protestors to handle their objection to abortion.

Planning is what it's all about.   Abortion reflects a lack of planning or a lack of proper planning on the mother's part.   This message of planning must be given to high school girls loud and clear for it is they, the girls who as women will give birth, not the men.

If women do not want to have babies they should have their fallopian tubes tied.

There is this life-long concern about the needy.   I do a lot of thinking about them.   Today I will hear a particular message of concern about the needy.

It's a beautiful Sunday morning.   I open my eyes and through the Venetian blinds I see the sun rising to greet me.   I'm not sure whether the birds with their chirping awakened me or the traffic in its onrush to arrive at some destination.   All seems well with the world.   But I am hardly out of dreamland.

I eat my breakfast, cereal with a cut-up banana and a cup of hot coffee, thinking about the day ahead.   There is reading I'd like to do, letters I need to write.   But first I will go to church.   I go to my closet, select what I will wear and pretty soon I'm off to hear a sermon.

On this particular Sunday, the minister admonishes the congregation to uncloak themselves of self-centeredness and reach out to the needy among us. His words are penetrating and selfishness and charity intermingle in the minds of the congregation.

Every Sunday is charity Sunday, in part, when the collection plate is passed around. But this day there is a special collection for the needy.

The needy are heavy upon all of our minds as we file out shaking hands with the minister and thanking him for an inspiring sermon.

I walk down the steps and onto the street pondering the words I have just heard. I remember the time when I was needy. The time when my second grade teacher gave me that pretty little dress and matching panties when she had kept me after school to clean the blackboard.

It's a very personal thing how each of us, with the money at our disposal, will deal with helping the less fortunate. I, and I believe most people who have a community concern, feel rewarded spiritually when lending a helping hand for someone less fortunate.

A week has passed. I wonder what the minister's sermon will be about this sprinkly breezy Sunday. I sit down to a dish of oatmeal and apricots, and a cup of hot chocolate.

I must leave early to pick up my mail from my Post Office Box. I unlock the Post Office door with my secret code and head towards my box. I witness what I have previously witnessed on my early morning visits to my Post Office Box. I see homeless people, with whatever possessions they have, sleeping or trying to sleep on the cold floor. Some kind soul had let them in. I thank God I never had to sleep on a Post Office floor.

And then I wonder where will those people on the Post Office floor eat breakfast, and then lunch, and dinner? Where will they sleep tonight, and tomorrow night, and the next night?

I don't look at their faces so I don't know if they're the same people I've seen before or not. Where did they come from? What is their background? I didn't ask any questions. I wonder what their stories would have been. Maybe they wouldn't have told me the truth had I asked. And, so, I go out to my car and drive to church.

Today's ministration is a sequel to last Sunday's sermon. We hear about kindness and the Good Samaritan. We must be a caring people.

I walk from the church determined to give more to charity. I get in my car and drive on Massachusetts Avenue west, pass the numerous embassies, and make a right on Wisconsin Avenue. As I drive north on Wisconsin Avenue, as I go through the Friendship Heights and Bethesda areas, I view the tall professional sky-reaching office buildings, now on Sunday, empty of their high-income lawyers, doctors, and other professionals and their staffs. They have beautiful multi-glass architecturally designed facades. They represent the wealth of America. I pass the elegant Hyatt Regency Hotel and continue on.

I pass the vast acreage on the right where the National Naval Medical Center is located and on my left is the National Institutes of Health.

At this point Wisconsin Avenue becomes Rockville Pike. A few blocks farther up the Pike I stop at the White Flint Mall to purchase an item on my list and have a bite to eat in the Mall Eatery.

Back in my car, I decide to take a drive through the Potomac subdivision where, as a real estate agent, I had listed and sold homes. It's such a beautiful area of expensive mansion-type homes to drive through.

Just having come from church and the sermon about the needy, I begin to think about the wealthy and how they became wealthy. Their station in life captivates my thoughts.

They may have had antecedents who worked hard, became wealthy, and passed the proverbial silver spoon on to them. And, they themselves may have worked hard to become wealthy.

Many of the wealthy of the world, the millionaires, those who strove for their level in the financial world, are truly appreciative of their plateau and express it in philanthropic ways.

On the other hand much of the wealth of the world becomes bottled up in extravagant ways or is thrown to the winds in senseless endeavors.

Most people are not born with a silver spoon in their mouth and must make their own way up whatever ladder they choose.

Every poor man should realize that with self-motivation, with goals, with the capabilities at his disposal, he can put his own efforts in motion to obtain a proverbial silver spoon to pass on to his own progeny.

There are a lot of silver spoons out there and it can be far more exciting finding one's own instead of coveting someone else's.

It has been wisely said: "Instead of waiting for your ship to come in, paddle your own canoe out to meet it." This pretty well sums up the entrepreneur's philosophy.

Many of the poor are a proud people. They aspire to greater income and achieve it. (I did it.) There are even those who, striving for that silver spoon, bypass the middle income level and arrive at the top. Many have risen from the bottom rung of the ladder to the top of their ladder through self-motivation.

Let's face it. We are born with different potential. This is something we really need to understand. How many of us will be an Einstein, a Nobel Prize winner, a great world leader, a renowned doctor, or a great scientist? We must accept ourselves as mother nature endowed us.

Hardly can we expect to be like Masoud Karkehabadi who, at 10 years of age, became a pre-med student with the possibility of becoming a physician at age 18.

We have to determine what our own abilities are. I once sat in a beauty parlor and was reading an article in a magazine about hospitals and operations while waiting for my hair to be done. I fainted while reading the article and when I came to they sent me home in a cab. Just reading about hospitals and blood was too much for me. So, even if I had had the finances to pursue a medical education I could never have become a doctor.

We have different abilities and potential and we have choices. We pursue different levels and kinds of education and, I believe, most of us set goals as to which ladder we want to climb and how far up the ladder we want to climb. Not everyone wants to climb to the top. And, of course, there isn't room at the top for everyone. One time when I was promoted I recommended a particular person to fill the job I was leaving. That person had no interest in being promoted to the job I was leaving. She was comfortable right where she was. So, we seek different levels of achievement.

Sadly, too many of the needy seem unaware of the need to set goals. They seem to be content with the status quo even though they seek help from others.

Government welfare, sad to say, has enrutted many to a permanent acceptance of the handout. They continue to be takers from the Government's, the taxpayers', bucket of goodwill and taxpayer dollars continue to roll in their direction. Too many of the poor wallow permanently in the acceptance of help from others without giving any thought to setting a goal to remove themselves from their plight.

Others can lend a hand but that hand shouldn't be looked on as a permanent fixture. Welfare funds taken from taxpayer dollars wind up in the pockets of too many people who plan their life so as to ensure being the recipient of such funds.

While we can't realistically expect to wipe out poverty completely, we can take steps in that direction by directing our efforts to more meaningful ways of caring for the needy than via the dole.

They must learn personal responsibility and their need to set goals for themselves so that they can become self-supporting.

Too many of the needy seem to be malnourished mentally when it comes to goal setting. They must be urged to set realistic goals for themselves so that they can escape from being encapsulated in the welfare system.

We can help them on an individual basis by determining in what direction their skills can take them and assist them in finding work requiring their particular skills.

The important thing is for them to get on a ladder, to work and earn money even though it may be little at the outset, and to seek advancement based on their capability.

One cannot allow one's self to be thrown when it seems one cannot reach his goal. One must press on and sometimes it is smart to switch goals.

Any career ladder carries with it a requirement of knowledge. We may be fortunate and possess the wherewithal to acquire an extensive number of years of higher education or we may spend many hours poring over books in the library to increase our knowledge. Or, we may resort to any number of ways to acquire knowledge. Learning is more important than how it is obtained.

Personality can play an important role in escaping poverty. Many have risen from the lowly rung of the economic ladder and achieved success because of personality. Personal drive and learning are definitely important but personality can provide an extra leverage. That is one reason why all those things I spoke of earlier in this book about the building of character in children are so important.

In an article in the PARADE MAGAZINE[*], August 9, 1992, written by Marvin Scott, we read about Florence Henderson's rise to success. The matriarch of the popular "The Brady Bunch" TV production, she was born in poverty and was ashamed of the hand-me-down dresses with holes in them that she wore to school. She used her talent and will to succeed, to rise above her circumstances. Not many have her talent. Each has to find his own. And, one has to capture the inner strength that she possessed and which carried her to a high plateau in her chosen field.

George Mitchell rose from humble beginnings to fill one of the most prestigious positions in the United States Congress, that of Senate Majority Leader.

James Roche worked in low-paying jobs to get through high school. He never went to college. In the 1960's he became a $700,000 a year Chairman of the Board of General Motors.

John Major rose from humble beginnings to be Prime Minister of Britain.

Sonny Bono's education ended at the high school level, yet he was elected Mayor of Palm Springs, California by the largest margin in the city's history. He balanced the city's budget, eliminated a $2,500,000 deficit without imposing new taxes, and was elected to be the Honorable Sonny Bono in the House of Representatives of the United States Congress. (Congressional Directory 1997-1998)

---

[*] Reprinted with permission from PARADE, copyright© 1992, and writer Marvin Scott.

And so we say "Hurrah" for those who succeed in spite of this, that, or the other, and we wish all men could have the same spirit, but we are realists and we know that there will always be the needy among us who have a problem negotiating the first step of a career ladder, and when they do there is the question of how much beyond that first step they can go.

It's a frame of mind that determines to a great degree how far up the ladder one will go in any avenue of his life. Accepting the status quo is a formula for stagnation.

There are many who are happy right where they are. This is no problem so long as they are not a burden to others. When others have to step in to provide the necessities for daily living it is then necessary to look for ways to convert the receiver into a self-provider.

We're on a mental ladder in life and we reach varying heights depending on a number of things. First, the inborn intellect. I do not believe that everyone is born with the same possibility for achievement. Consider Masoud Karkehabadi of whom I have already mentioned. Minds are different and he is proof of that.

The poor who seek help must analyze their situation, decide where they are on the mental and economic scale, and search out ways for up and out of their plight.

Philosophy of overcoming the down-and-out life, no matter how well formulated, fails to catch on with too many of the needy. And, so, too many of them continue to be a part of our society. I know what it's like to have been poor and so do millions of others. We need to draw more currently poor people into the "have been poor" group.

The need for charity can best be determined at the community level, and it is at that level that welfare programs can be administered most effectively. Many factors are involved which vary from

127

community to community, the cost of food and housing, the availability of volunteers, etc.

Three major organizations have been needy-friendly over the years: the RED CROSS, THE SALVATION ARMY, and the UNITED WAY. There are many organizations the mission of which is to help the needy, but these are the major ones.

The RED CROSS is best known for the work it does in disaster areas around the world whether in war or peace and there is long-standing admiration for its work.

Also, there can be only accolades for THE SALVATION ARMY. It has done a magnificent amount of commendable charity work over many years in helping the poor and the destitute. It is described as the nation's largest Charity in FORBES magazine of October 29, 2001.

Both the RED CROSS and THE SALVATION ARMY are fully committed to helping the needy, each in its own way.

The UNITED WAY functions differently. It serves as a *middleman* by collecting funds which it distributes to hundreds of organizations, *many of which have nothing to do with helping the poor.*

Most of the organizations which receive money from the UNITED WAY use the funds for other purposes than to provide the poor with food, clothing, and shelter. The UNITED WAY collects funds for animals, the performing arts, museums and memorials, sports, worldwide programs, research, schools and religious connections, and numerous other programs having nothing to do with providing the needy with food, clothing, and shelter.

Incident to giving to the UNITED WAY, you can designate for which organization under its umbrella you wish your money to be given. If you wish your money to be used for food, clothing, and/or shelter for the needy, then you should designate an organization which serves this purpose. But the full amount of your gift will not be given to the program of your choice. There is a cut for the middleman, the UNITED WAY.

*By donating directly to the program of your choice you remove the UNITED WAY as a middleman.* Thus, more of your money is put to its intended use.

Certainly, organizational efforts to help the poor and needy are important, and donating to the extent we can to these organizations is to be encouraged. However, to the extent we can perform a beneficial service by helping the needy on a volunteer one-to-one basis, or helping the needy through local community, neighborhood, or religious group efforts we should do so, never forgetting to realize the importance of not only providing basic needs, but also doing what we can to get the needy on a self-providing track.

I remember the time that our house burned down when I was a little girl and we were living in Adrian, Michigan, and how the neighbors gave us temporary shelter. Wherever there is a need we should lend a helping hand. There are so many ways in which we can do this. It isn't necessarily a hand over of money. We can show kindness in many ways. There are many types of needs to which we can respond in a positive way.

We can best help a person who seems stagnated in poverty by getting answers to the following questions. What are his skills? What is his education? What efforts has he personally made to find work? Where has he applied for work? Why does he think he hasn't found a job? What kind of work has he done in the past? Does he have any source of income or does he have any money in the bank? And, most of all, has he set any goals for himself and has he pursued any of the goals?

He might be a hobo and thriving on that kind of life. Some, I believe, are so into hobo living that they really enjoy it and have no desire to leave that mode of life. But, let's assume he's redeemable and we want to help him find a means of income, a job. Asking the above questions is a starting point.

This inquiry into his personal situation can be done best on a one-to-one basis either as a result of personal interest in a particular person or as part of an organizational or state-sponsored effort to help the poor.

Just pouring out money is not enough. Our efforts must be to get them on a work ladder. And, we can help them find that work ladder.

We should be ever mindful of the needy and do what we can to assist them in not only their immediate situation but more importantly to get them on a track for the future.

The needy are only one of a number of people problems in our society. There are those who aren't able to live their full life with the brain in the same normal condition as it was when they were born. Their brain has become dysfunctional and they can't function normally. They become insane.

The mind of an insane person can be likened to a machine that is out of control because some of its parts malfunction. Would we trust such a machine? Of course not. Nor should we trust a person with a malfunctioning brain to be on our streets.

They live in a whole different mental world. I once visited a patient in an insane asylum, a person I knew very well. I tried to communicate with the patient but the patient spoke weirdly of nothing relating to reality. *It's like they live in a strange eerie dream world, and the exit door from that strange eerie dream world is locked.* They stay in their crazy dream world and are permanently locked out of the real world.

Insane people commit horrible crimes. They should be placed in an insane asylum and kept there.

We have too many victims caused by mentally ill people. We should confine those who are mentally ill so as to prevent them from criminal activity.

They shouldn't be allowed to leave the mental facility after they are placed there.

On June 30, 2000, there were 17,354 criminals receiving mental health treatment in state correctional facilities. Also on that date an estimated 151,500 state inmates were in mental health therapy/counseling programs; 114,200 inmates were receiving psychotropic medications; and 19,100 were in 24-hour care. (U.S. Dept. of Justice, Office of Justice Programs, Bureau of Justice Statistics, Special Report, Mental Health Treatment in State Prisons, 2000, NCJ 188215). The mentally ill should be in an insane asylum with no revolving door, not in prison facilities.

They commit blood-curdling crimes and should be kept in an insane asylum away from a world they can't function properly in, away from people they can harm because of their out-of-control minds.

Will we place insane people in an insane asylum or will we let the victims pile up?

There are those who become angry, commit crime, and claim temporary insanity. What they really did was get angry and let their anger get out of control.

Anger has no relationship to insanity. We are all capable of becoming angry. Every normal person is capable of becoming angry. How we handle anger depends on the controls we have put in place in our own mind.

Anger can have disastrous results and is the reason for many crimes. It is so important to hold anger in tow so that crimes will not be committed.

Angry words alone can kill. Unbelievable but I personally saw it happen. No gun or other instrument of death, just a mean and ugly tongue caused the death.

It happened in the Internal Revenue Service Training Division. There was a meeting called by the Director of the Division which was attended by his staff, Branch Chiefs, and all other employees in the Division.

One of the employees in the meeting was angry with her Branch Chief about something that could and should have been resolved in his private office. Instead, the employee confronted her Branch Chief with very caustic criticism in the meeting. Her criticism became a speech from her place in the audience.

All others in attendance were shocked. The Branch Chief was a highly respected person. Why didn't she talk to him in his office instead of engaging in this mean diatribe in the presence of all employees of the Division? We wondered. What she was saying was mean talk, not searching for answers talk. It was not asking questions or making suggestions. It was lambasting.

After the meeting the Branch Chief, overcome with hurt, went directly to a conference room and dropped dead of a heart attack.

There was absolutely no doubt in anyone's mind as to why the Branch Chief had a heart attack and died. The employee's angry words had killed him.

Communication should take place in a civilized manner. There is never an excuse for angry words. Anything can be said civilly.

Displaying anger is an uncivilized part of us. We can be angry but we don't have to display it. Confrontation should be handled with composure and controlled dialogue. If composure and dialogue don't work then disassociate yourself from the source of the problem.

There was the fellow who, angry because a man stepped on his foot and didn't say he was sorry, murdered the guy who had stepped on his foot, and was sent to prison for the murder.

Murdering an offender, fighting him, whatever, out of anger only acknowledges that you lack self-control.

Sure, the offender should have learned long before becoming an adult how to treat people decently. We know, however, that many don't know what decency is all about. They go around stepping on people's toes one way or another. They stumble through life offending others.

The man whose foot was stepped on was naturally teed off and angry when no words of "I'm sorry" were heard. There was, however, a far more intelligent way of handling the situation than murdering the guy, and going to prison.

Any self-respecting person would be hurt if someone were to step on his foot and not at least say "I'm sorry." But, murdering the guy is not very intelligent.

How to handle such a situation without letting the brain boil over with anger is the art of understanding what leadership is all about and having the wisdom to hold anger in tow, keeping anger in the brain and not exposing it.

The person who stepped on the foot was the leader in the situation because he started it. It's his game. He made the first move. He planted the seed.

It's stupid to follow him in his game. Confronted by such a person, you have an opportunity to put him on a whole different track by exerting your own leadership.

You take over the controls. You be the leader in your own game. Ask him what's bothering him. Maybe you can give him some help which he surely needs. He's headed for disaster and he definitely needs help. You, with your leadership, can turn him around to the world of decency. That way you will have rendered a valuable service of kindness to your fellowman, you won't wind up in a court of law, and you won't go to prison.

133

The other guy will be a better person walking our streets because of your leadership and kindness. It would be a step forward for civilization.

We must live on a platform of self-containment no matter how the world whirls around us. Only by doing so can we be master of our own self.

There are those who carry into adulthood the mental baggage of an unpleasant childhood and they vent their anger about their unpleasant childhood by stepping on people's toes in one way or another.

The grief of the past eats at their sense of well-being and they indulge in self-pity. Many times that self-pity turns into anger which they vent against others. They commit crime and blame it on a traumatic childhood.

Those who carry their childhood problems into adulthood are doomed to a life of unnecessary turbulence.

Many didn't have the hugs and kisses they craved as a child. They were mistreated or had heart-rending experiences, or didn't have proper training. They entertain thoughts about what happened in yesteryears and reflect anger about it in the way they treat their fellowman in adulthood. This can be disastrous for both themselves and others with whom they come in contact.

Many have had childhood difficulties which could have doomed them to a life of suffering because of carry-over grief, but instead chose to put their grief in a mental closet and throw away the key. I threw away the key and I think anyone else can.

Negative thoughts about one's childhood must be put in a mental closet which must not be opened to explode. We must close the door on the negative of the past for we have no power to change it. It will be as it was forever. We must live for now and the future.

To expect only roses to be strewn in one's path is unrealistic. There will be many disappointments and discouraging moments throughout life and sometimes we think we can't make it. Sometimes we must ford the waters of seeming impossibilities to reach a solution.

Yesterdays can never be returned. When something happens affecting our lives adversely, it has already occurred. It is part of the past. The past is gone forever. We can never return to it. But we can make things different in the future, or at least try to. We should always steer our lives toward a better tomorrow instead of grieving about the past.

Dragging unpleasant memories from childhood into adulthood, clinging to those woes, and letting them affect one negatively, deprives one of happiness as an adult. Happiness follows letting go of the past and concentrating on today and tomorrow.

So, I say, step into the sunlight and let the grief of the past fade into oblivion. There is much happiness to be found. Just look for it. And make it.

We must realize the importance of our role as a citizen. As such we are, or should be, concerned about our laws, local and national. Are they fair or aren't they? Do they or do they not protect us? Are they written in order to protect the criminal?

America provides a number of protections for criminals in the U.S. Constitution. The U.S. Constitution expresses no concern about victims, it only expresses an interest in the welfare of criminals. And, it does this quite profusely.

Regardless of the severity of his crime, he is many times let off because of this, that, or the other technicality. And, there are many technicalities that can result in freedom for the most violent criminal.

No matter how the victim was tortured and died struggling and pleading for mercy, no matter how beastly the murderer committed his crime, no matter the kidnapper's treatment of his victim, no matter the violation of one's person by rape or otherwise the criminal is treated as though he were the victim under our present laws and this is wrong.

Too many criminals are freed on some technicality. If one has been proven guilty of a crime, no technicality should free him. Criminals must pay for their crimes under a fair justice system.

So many times they have been freed on a technicality and they said: "Thank God for the technicality." It's a door to freedom for the vilest of criminals. This is not right. It's a bouquet of roses and a hail-fellow and well-done as the criminal walks to freedom.

Only if he can bring his deceased victim back to life or undo the harm he has otherwise wrought should he be freed and since it is impossible for him to do this he should pay the penalty and not be let off on a technicality.

No technicality should set a convicted criminal free. He should be able to obtain freedom only if it is later found that he did not commit the crime.

Whoever is guilty of the technical error should be punished but the criminal should not be set free because of a technical error.

The 4th Amendment to the U.S. Constitution reads:

"The right of the people to be secure in their persons, houses, papers, and effects, against unreasonable searches and seizures, shall not be violated, and no warrants shall issue but upon probable cause, supported by oath or affirmation, and particularly describing the place to be searched, and the persons or things to be seized."

There are those who commit crime and are set free because a search warrant wasn't issued. Our system of justice is bent on ways to free the criminal. There are cases in which a search warrant shouldn't be required, cases in which an immediate search is justified.

A man was pulled over for speeding by two state troopers. They asked if they could look in his van. The driver said they could then sprang open the lock and ran away. Inside the trunk was the body of a man who had been shot five times. The driver was caught. In his apartment the suspect told them where to look for the murder weapon and it was recovered. The man was convicted and was sentenced to 45 years to life. The search of the man's apartment had been made without a search warrant.[*] With the evidence of a crime found in the van a search warrant should not have been required.

The 5th Amendment to the U.S. Constitution says:

"...nor shall be compelled in any criminal case to be a witness against himself..."

This mandate allows the criminal to remain silent about his involvement in a crime. It throws a protective shield around him. This is just one example of how our forefathers went to extremes to protect the criminal.

Defense lawyering is all about hiding detrimental information and gaining freedom for the client no matter the seriousness of the crime. Our justice system should be about bringing out the truth, not hiding it.

Permitting the accused to remain silent is a major hindrance to getting all the truth before the jury. It slams the door on vital information. This is not justice. In the interest of true justice, the accused should be required to speak for himself.

---

[*] Reprinted with permission from PARADE, copyright© 1996 and writer Bernard Gavzer.

Firsthand information from the accused could be far more meaningful than secondhand information provided by a defense lawyer who knows only what his client chooses to tell him. You can be sure that the accused will be very selective in what he tells his defense lawyer.

Also, common sense tells us that the defense lawyer doesn't want to know the whole truth if it would militate against his client.

The defense lawyer is skilled in the art of ferreting out ways to lead the accused to freedom or a light sentence. He will exert a gargantuan effort in trying to keep truth that is detrimental to his client hidden.

The 6th Amendment to the U.S. Constitution says:

"...the accused shall enjoy the right to a speedy... trial..."

A speedy trial is not always possible because of a pileup of cases to be tried.

The court's log should be kept intact and all cases tried. A pileup of criminals to be tried is clear evidence that there are too many criminals because of too weak laws. Freed for the reason that a speedy trial did not take place, the criminal figures crime is easy to get away with and so he goes out and commits more crime.

One of the two 18-year-old men charged with the killing of basketball Superstar Michael Jordan's father should have been in prison for a previous crime but had been let out of prison because the 6th Amendment to the U.S. Constitution requires a speedy trial which had not taken place. (As reported in The Washington Post August 17, 1993)

A man arrested in the stabbing of a man and the rape and stabbing of his 79-year-old grandmother had been released from jail the day before the crimes because of delays in trying him on earlier charges.

He figured the courts are too busy to try him so why not commit more crimes. (As reported in The Washington Post May 24, 1994)

Anyone charged with murder or other bodily harm should be confined until trial takes place. Never should a person be freed because trial hadn't taken place.

Too many trials for judges to handle is clear evidence that there is too much crime and that action is desperately needed to reduce crime. The Bill of Rights with its freedom doors is responsible for so much crime.

The 6th Amendment to the U.S. Constitution says:

"...the accused shall... enjoy the right... to have compulsory process for obtaining witnesses in his favor."

Such witnesses should consist of only those who have knowledge about the particular crime. They should not be character witnesses. Too many presumed-to-be upright people have committed crime.

Certainly we would expect the President of the UNITED WAY to be an upright person. William Aramony, President of the UNITED WAY for over 20 years, was convicted for using contributor money for his personal pleasure.

He had been eligible for a pension of over $4,000,000. This is outrageous. Do those who donate to the UNITED WAY know that they help make the President of the UNITED WAY a multimillionaire? I doubt that they do but they should know it.

Because of the way he used contributor money he actually received a lesser pension. But the pension had been there for him had he not been convicted of squandering money from the charity.

The treasurer of one of America's largest churches was found guilty of embezzling $1.5 million dollars from the church and failing to pay the proper income taxes.

The highly respected chairman and principal owner of a bank was found guilty of using $25,000,000 of the bank's funds to live an extravagant life style in Europe.

A high ranking employee of the United Food and Commercial Workers International Union used $1.75 million of the Union's funds to buy a sumptuous home.

The former Executive Director of a Housing Finance Agency was charged with spending over $230,000 from the Agency's funds for personal pleasure.

No matter the standing one has had in his community and other relationships, if he commits a crime he no longer is worthy of being applauded for his previous standing.

The 6th Amendment to the U.S. Constitution says:

"...the accused shall... have the assistance of counsel for his defense."

Because the defense lawyer goes beyond counseling by taking on the role of spokesman for the accused in the courtroom, the jury is deprived of direct testimony from the accused.

The services of the defense lawyer in the courtroom should be limited to counseling the defendant. The jury needs to hear from the accused directly.

The 6th Amendment is interesting in that it uses the word "enjoy." It says:

"In all criminal prosecutions, the accused shall enjoy the right to a speedy and public trial... to have compulsory process for obtaining witnesses in his favor, and to have the assistance of counsel for his defense."

Why did our forefathers want the criminal to "*enjoy?*" Did our forefathers want criminals to enjoy the fact that they, our forefathers, provided so much protection for them in The Bill of Rights? Our forefathers certainly were intent on making everything favorable for the criminal. They say nothing about not creating victims, it's all about the criminal enjoying himself in spite of his crime. The 6th Amendment needs to be revised. The word "enjoy" is inappropriate.

The 8th Amendment to the U.S. Constitution reads:

"Excessive bail shall not be required, nor excessive fines imposed, nor cruel and unusual punishment inflicted."

Our forefathers spoke only of comfort and compassion for the criminal. No words are spoken of concern for the victim, the fact that the victim was savagely raped and/or murdered, or that other disastrous things happened to victims. Their concern was all about making things comfortable for the criminal, and they express this very clearly.

In effect, our forefathers said, no matter how horrendous the crime, we must treat the criminal kindly.

Our criminals are treated with a piece of cake. It's time to change this. There is too much sympathy for the criminal. We must concentrate on reducing the number of victims and provide adequate punishment to accomplish this.

Indeed, our U.S. Constitution has much to say about kindly treatment for the criminal but has not one word to say about victims and how there should be such punishment as is necessary to prevent there being so many victims.

Why did they not express concern about victims? Why did they not even mention victims? Victims are brutally murdered, very brutally murdered, and harmed in many other ways. Let's take the love and sympathy away from the criminal and give it to the victim.

And let's make the punishment of the criminal such as will deter others from committing crime.

Sympathy, leniency, and freedom for the criminal are abundant in our justice system. Gargantuan efforts to protect the criminal, going to extremes to do so, have freed the criminal from fear of what the consequences of his crime will be. America is the land of freedom, and certainly for the criminal.

In today's world, the criminal's mind works like this: Go to prison, get all that care, watch television, read in the prison library, enjoy the prison's other benefits, behave, get out of prison and commit more crime. At least this is the way it is with too many criminals. Where's the punishment? It's merely confinement with many benefits connected with the confinement. Let's introduce some meaningful punishment. It's long overdue.

Americans age 12 or older experienced approximately 24,200,000 crimes in 2001 according to a National Crime Victimization Survey. 5,700,000 were violent crimes including 84,000 rapes.[*] This great number tells us that the punishment on the books doesn't deter crime.

There have been 27 Amendments to the U.S. Constitution. There should be another Amendment declaring the Bill of Rights replaced with provisions that will provide whatever punishment is necessary to reduce the number of victims.

We should not have criminal sympathizers in leadership and decision-making roles.

A Supreme Court Justice opposed the death sentence claiming that it treats members of the human race as non-humans, that even the vilest criminal remains a human being possessed of common human dignity. Did he not think that the victims were human beings

---

[*] SOURCE: U.S. Department of Justice, Office of Justice Programs, Bureau of Justice Statistics, NCJ 194610 September 2002.

possessed of common human dignity? His sympathy was on the wrong side of the grave.

Sounds like this Supreme Court Justice cares not one iota for victims. Where is the dignity spoken of by the Supreme Court Justice as it relates to a criminal, a murderer?

Was this Supreme Court Justice saying that he considers the Manson Family and Jeffrey Dahmer were possessed of common human dignity? Really? Who in their right mind would agree to that?

Is this the kind of person we want to serve on the Supreme Court? Was he questioned adequately at the hearing conducted by the United States Senate before his nomination was confirmed? Or, could it be that those who confirmed his nomination were in agreement with him.

Criminals seek sympathy from any source they can get it. Sympathy grew for a murderer on death row who had confessed to the rape and murder of a 15-year-old girl and the murder of her mother. He had been on death row for almost 12 years and was scheduled to be executed when efforts were made to spare his life because he studied law while in prison and took steps to benefit other inmates.

This double murderer and rapist had built up such expertise in law while in prison that one of the cases he initiated went to the Supreme Court and resulted in a benefit for prisoners.

It was felt that because he had educated himself (in prison while on death row) and had been instrumental in helping other inmates to escape punishment or receive extra benefits, that the Governor should have mercy on him and permit him to escape execution or receive extra benefits.

It occurs to me that any sympathy should be for the 15-year-old girl he raped and murdered and for the girl's mother he murdered.

Turning his life around while in prison (How easy it is behind locked doors and surrounded by guards) and doing something to help other prisoners is too late. He committed the crime and should pay the penalty.

If he was concerned about others, he should not have raped a 15-year-old girl and murdered her and her mother. Why didn't he do something to ease the pain of their family? Helping other inmates can in no way offset those horrible crimes. Since he could not bring the mother and daughter back to life and remove the trauma caused by his crimes, there should be no sympathy for him. He had no compassion for his victims so there should be no sympathy for him.

Instead of reading law books in prison, he should have suffered physical punishment. Why is he better than his victims? They suffered, so he should suffer as a consequence.

It's shocking that there are upright citizens who sympathize with criminals. They even marry or become friends with prisoners because they feel sorry for them. Disaster can follow such relationships.

There was the 55-year-old widow who yearned for companionship and, with a motherly instinct, began corresponding with prison inmates. When one with whom she had been corresponding was paroled he went to live with her. A week later she was found beaten to death and the parolee was charged with the murder. He had no appreciation for her motherliness. Instead, he viciously murdered her. (As reported in The Washington Post January 14, 1995)

There are those who object to the Death Sentence because of the words in the Ten Commandments in the Bible which say "Thou shalt not kill."

Those who object to the Death Sentence because of those words in the Ten Commandments should read the Bible further and they would find what the Bible says should happen to those who do kill another person.

*The Bible says those who kill should themselves be killed.* Read the following Bible verses which say murderers should be killed:

"Whoso sheddeth man's blood,
by man shall his blood be shed."
(Genesis: Chapter 9, Verse 6)

"He that smiteth a man so that he
die shall be surely put to death."
(Exodus: Chapter 21, Verse 12)

"And if he smite him... so that he
die, he is a murderer. The murderer
shall be put to death."
(Numbers; Chapter 35, Verse 16)

"Moreover, ye shall take no
satisfaction for the life of a
murderer, which is guilty of death,
but he shall be surely put to death."
(Numbers: Chapter 35, Verse 31)

And, so, the Bible says: Thou shalt not kill but goes on to say if you do kill your life will be taken because of the murder you committed.

The most heinous crimes of all are those having to do with another person's body. There should be the Death Sentence for not only murder but also for rape, child molestation, and kidnapping. (Domestic violence varies. It should be handled appropriately.) If they commit one of these crimes they themselves would be asking for the Death Sentence.

Prisons should be used for only those who have committed crime against another person's body and those who should be incarcerated for national or other security reasons.

Those guilty of murder, rape, child molestation, or kidnapping should be given 1½ years in prison before being executed. This would be a gift to the criminal. It's a year and a half more than he gave his victim.

Those who think the electric chair, etc, a horrible way to die should instead consider the horrible death or vicious treatment of the victim. Let's stop pushing the victim out of the picture with so much sympathy for the criminal. It's the victims we should be concerned about, not the criminals who made them victims. Criminals can surely say "God bless America" because it is so good to them.

The extent of kindness to anyone sent to Death Row should be to allow him to choose the method of execution, i.e., lethal injection, lethal gas, electrocution, hanging, or firing squad.

When execution takes place, instead of banners being carried outside the execution chambers saying: "No death penalty" such banners should read: "One more less to fear" or "You did the crime now take the punishment."

Sentencing for crimes that have nothing to do with a person's body but rather have to do with possessions should not involve prison time. Prison is too easy an escape for those who rob or commit arson, fraud, or embezzlement. They should be punished in a more meaningful manner.

Those guilty of these crimes need to repay their victims. If he doesn't have funds to repay his victim and doesn't work and have a salary which can be garnished to repay his victim, he should be sentenced to road work or other public work and funds taken from his earnings to repay his victim. This would be more appropriate and meaningful punishment.

He should be required to repay his victim in some manner. Perhaps borrow the money for repayment, but it should be repaid.

If an insurance company pays his victim, he should repay the insurance company.

We should move vigorously in the direction of crime prevention and meaningful punishment would help to do this.

The centuries-old Bill of Rights constituting the first ten Amendments to the U.S. Constitution is outdated for today's world and is desperately in need of replacement.

During the twentieth century we witnessed a great many innovations which have benefited mankind far more than had ever before been imagined.

Now we need to turn our attention to our justice system and change it to meet the needs of today's world. Replacing the Bill of Rights with laws to meet the needs of today's world should be at the top of our agenda. Victims, victims, victims, millions of victims, have created an urgency to do this. Or, are we going to continue to be more interested in the comfort of the criminal and let the victims pile up.

The courtroom is the centerpiece of our American justice system. Justice is not always rendered because of weaknesses in how the trial is conducted.

Winning the case is more important to the defense attorney than whether justice is served. Crime is the caviar and lofty living of defense lawyers. They are paid handsomely for their efforts to gain freedom for their clients. A reputation for winning cases can result in the defense lawyer getting high profile cases and earning huge sums of money for his services. Reducing crime and implementing a more meaningful justice system would dip into the defense lawyer's pocket, but we must reduce crime. It's gotten way out of control and we must reduce it. We can't wait any longer to do something about the vast amount of crime in America.

On the other hand, the prosecutor who assumes guilt wants to win the case because it enhances his position.

Both the defense lawyer and the prosecutor want to be the winner.

A meaningful trial must be about bringing out all the truth in the case and not about the defense lawyer or the prosecutor winning for self-aggrandizement.

We need to dispense with the defense lawyer as spokesman by confining his responsibility to counseling his client as provided for in the 6th Amendment, and we need to dispense with the prosecutor who assumes guilt.

In lieu thereof, to preside over the trial, there should be appointed a JUSTICE COORDINATOR.

Whereas under our present system the prosecutor assumes guilt and the defense attorney assumes not guilty, the JUSTICE COORDINATOR would not prejudge guilt or innocence, and, therefore, would not have a case to win or lose. His sole responsibility would be to get all the facts for the jury's consideration. And, based on the jury's finding of guilt or innocence, only the accused would win or lose.

The jury needs all the facts and the amount of facts made available to the jury would be maximized under a JUSTICE COORDINATOR since there would be direct testimony by the accused in the courtroom with questions put to the accused by the JUSTICE COORDINATOR.

Witnesses would, of course, also testify. If DNA or other tests are to be made they should be ordered in such a way that the provider and witness speaking to the results of such test(s) would not be beholden to anyone who is a part of the trial. This would avoid a client relationship whereby such provider would feel obligated to provide a certain result.

Following the testimonies of all parties, questions which may arise should be given to the JUSTICE COORDINATOR to get answers to.

Jury members should then have an opportunity to meet with the JUSTICE COORDINATOR to ask any questions they may have, some of which may result in further questioning of trial participants. After having listened carefully to all the testimonies and obtaining answers to its questions, if any, the jury would convene to determine guilty or not guilty.

The sentence handed down by the judge should be one that is mandated by law for the particular crime. In other words, the sentence should be based on the crime alone and should have nothing to do with the stature of the person who has been charged or with the judge's heartstrings.

Only by standardizing sentences can we wipe out the vast amount of inequity and unfairness which occurs in sentencing.

Establishing the role of JUSTICE COORDINATOR would be a major step towards implementing a meaningful and fair justice system.

A problem which would remain and cannot logically be solved is that jury members, no matter how carefully selected, each has built-in personal feelings about life, about right and wrong, and about many other things which are reflected in their decision about guilt or innocence.

It is recognition of these ingrained feelings that makes difficult the voir dire conducted by professional jury member selectors who are engaged to identify those persons deemed most likely to arrive at a decision of guilty or not guilty.

If all minds were fair there would be no need for professional jury member selectors to be engaged in the process of selecting jury members.

Regardless of the answers given by potential jurors on a pre-trial questionnaire, the decision of guilty or not guilty can still be influenced by the jurors' like or dislike for participants in the trial.

149

There are serious weaknesses in the jury system.

As long as we have the jury system we will be faced with the heartstrings of the jurors. The only solution is to replace the jury with God and, of course, this is not possible.

So, complete justice in the courtroom is not likely to ever be achieved, but we should take whatever steps to improve it that we can.

First, we should concentrate on reducing crime so that there will not be so much activity in our courtrooms.

We could start by getting answers from criminals as to why they committed crime. I'm sure there are many reasons.

We could find answers by requiring each one who is sentenced to state in writing why he committed his crime. The answers could lead to some solutions.

I wonder how many criminals had a religious background and committed crime in spite of their religious learnings. This is assuming that all religions teach brotherly love.

Religious establishments should be a bulwark in keeping man on a good citizenship track. Whether Buddhism, Christianity, Hinduism, Islamism (Muslim), Judaism, Shintoism, Taoism, Zoroastrianism, or whatever the religion, it can have a major impact on society through its sermonistic and moralistic counseling and should be Government's ally in crime prevention, though not officially.

Religion, whatever it may be, is all about directing one's life. Just as beauty is in the mind of the beholder, so it is with religion, that who or what is worshipped represents the supreme power in the mind of the worshipper.

We hear God, we hear Allah, we hear Ahura Mazda, we hear Buddha... Let's agree that there is only one God and that we can call him anything we please. I am not going to suggest what we call him for that's up to each individual.

I doubt that any of us would want to entertain a thought that there is more than one God. If there were more than one God I can see the Gods fighting among themselves as to which one is entitled to be called God. The heavens would be torn asunder with their fighting. If we believe in God, it's a matter of what each one of us thinks our God expects of us. I would hope it would include brotherly love.

No one has ever seen their God. Certainly he isn't mortal so he wouldn't be like man. Man is subject to death and God isn't, so he would not have a body which functions like man's. God is the mighty indescribable one who always was and always will be. I won't ask what kind of body God has or where God came from. There are no answers.

We say God is in heaven, in paradise. No one has ever come back from the place called heaven so regardless of what is written we really don't know what the so-called heaven is like. We know what man has written in the holy books but they who wrote about heaven had never been there. They wrote about what they think heaven is like.

And then there is hell that is supposed to be ruled by Satan. Now, where is hell? No one has ever come back from there either.

Now, I'm not trying to tear anyone's belief apart. I think we should look at God and Satan in a different way.

Since no one has ever come back from heaven or hell and can't speak about either place from a personal experience, instead of concentrating on heaven and hell, we should turn our thoughts to how we live our life on this earth. We should concentrate on how we live our life on earth and let the afterlife be whatever it is. After all, that is what heaven and hell are all about, a place to go based on how we *live our life on earth.* We should love one another, help one another, and never do harm to another.

Let's agree that God represents all that is good and that Satan represents that which is evil. Our basic concern then should be about Good and Evil. So, it's Go(o)d and (d)evil.

Our overall mission on earth should be to promote peace and goodness among its inhabitants. No matter where we live on earth we are all human beings and that should be our focus.

We should all, as human beings, no matter where we live on earth or to what heritage we were born, be free to pursue our own destiny, being a slave to no one.

America's period of slavery is a black mark on its history.

It is important to understand that the American government did not buy Africans to be slaves. Our American government, deeming it wrong for some of its citizens to have slaves, freed the slaves. It's a shame that it took a war to do so. The contention that we in today's world should be held responsible for what happened in past generations in ridiculous.

No one in the United States today had anything to do with slavery. We didn't live then and we are in no way responsible for what happened then. It's what happens on our own watch that we can be held responsible for.

Those in Africa who sold their own people for slavery and those who bought them are no longer living.

Those in today's world who seek recompense because their antecedents were slaves are thinking in the wrong direction. It is their antecedents who were slaves, not them. As a result of their ancestors they are now enjoying the American life. And, I assume they are happy to be Americans or do they wish their ancestors had not been sold for slavery under which circumstances they would be in Africa today.

Whether or not it is a blessing for descendants of slaves to be Americans, no blessing is worth a preexistence of slavery.

We must move forward in a spirit of human kindness and equality. Today should be our focus, not yesterday.

Africa is wrought with many ethnic and economic problems. The tribal wars send many to refugee camps and many to their death. The average per capita income of Africa's nations is probably the lowest in the world.

The Affirmative Action movement for black people is demeaning and degrading. It implies inferiority. It is about giving one race priority over another. The Civil War was fought to end discrimination.

Black men rise up their career ladders and many rise to the top of their career ladders. Some of our most prominent citizens are African Americans.

Booker T. Washington, a freed slave, showed early on that the black man is capable of rising to a position of prominence. He was named President of Tuskegee Institute[*] and authored several books. He is truly a great man in America's history.

Even though now deceased, Booker T. Washington is an inspiration to all of any color. His fortitude, brain power, and professionalism are what we admire.

If you'd like an experience that will touch your heart and soul with love, respect, and an understanding of fortitude, go to Roanoke,

---

[*] Tuskegee Institute National Historic Site in Alabama is located on the campus of the school Booker T. Washington founded in 1881 and is still in operation today.

Virginia, drive east on Route 24 and south on Route 122 to the plantation where Booker T. Washington lived as a slave in a shelter with a dirt floor.

If you visit the plantation where he lived as a slave, you cannot help but stand in awe of this wonderful man because of what he accomplished in his 59 years on this earth. He didn't shed tears in self-pity. Instead, he made something of himself, furthered possibilities for the enrichment of his fellowmen and is endeared by all America. The Booker T. Washington National Monument[*] is administered by the National Park Service, U.S. Department of the Interior.

Booker T. Washington made something of himself in spite of his circumstances. Every man can do the same.

African-Americans are elected to be Senators and Representatives in our United States Congress and to State legislative bodies. They become Mayors and State Attorneys. They set up their own offices as doctors and lawyers. They serve admirably as TV anchormen. They fill the role of professor and are teachers in our schools.

Richard Parsons emerged to a pivotal corporate position with Time Warner, a role for which he proved to be highly capable of filling.

Clarence Thomas spent no time in self-pity on his way up his ladder. He became a Justice on the Supreme Court of the United States of America. He didn't bemoan the fact that he is black. He thought of himself as an American with the opportunity to make himself what he wanted to be. He concentrated on diligently preparing himself for each rung of the ladder on his way up. With inner strength he made himself to be the man he is, one qualified to sit as an Associate Justice on the Supreme Court of the United States of America.

---

[*] A brochure can be obtained by calling 1(540) 721-2094.

Colin Powell rose to the powerful position of Chairman of the Joint Chiefs-of-Staff in our Defense Department and later became Secretary of State.

L. Douglas Wilder was elected to be Governor of the State of Virginia because not only was he right on the issues as viewed by the majority of Virginia's voters, but also because of his professionalism, stature, and statesmanlike composure. He, the people decided, was the most qualified for the Governorship.

Those who serve in high office, regardless of the color of their skin, must serve all citizens equally without preferential treatment for any one color.

Dr. Martin Luther King, Jr. was so highly respected that following his death a "Dr. Martin Luther King, Jr. Day" was added to our calendar as a Federal Legal Public Holiday. Even President Abraham Lincoln who brought about the freeing of the slaves doesn't have a Federal Legal Public Holiday named for him.

Equality must be reflected in our laws and law enforcement. A member of the United States Congress urged legislation to permit death row inmates to use statistics to challenge their sentences as racially biased. Statistics showing that 89% of defendants are African-American or Hispanic were used by the Congressman to justify his contention that special consideration should be given to the racial factor.[*]

Preposterous!!! This is racism pure and simple. To permit defendants to use race to challenge a death sentence or any other sentence is absurd and totally against the principle of equal justice for all.

Sentences must be based on the crime and not on the color of one's skin.

---

[*] SOURCE: The Washington Post, March 16, 1994 and July 18, 1994. Articles by Washington Post Staff Writer Kenneth J. Cooper.

Alice Vaeth

    The scales of justice must not be tipped in any direction by racist or ethnic motives.  They must provide for equal treatment for all guilty of a particular crime.

    It's the nature of the crime that should make the difference in sentencing, never the color of the skin.

    America must be ever vigilant to ensure equal justice for all.

    We should remove all those tags from people.  Let African-American people be Americans.  Let Spanish-American people be Americans. Let Asian-American people be Americans, etc.  Let's make all Americans a part of the American Pie instead of each being a separate kind of cookie.  Let the American Pie replace the rainbow philosophy.

    A foundation of commonality to ensure a unified America must be found for all groups to conform to.

    We can have differences.  The important thing is that our differences don't interfere with civilian harmony.

    America is a grand mixture of humanity.  It has citizens and non-citizens who have come from all over the world.  No other country in the world experiences the influx of immigrants to the extent that America does.

    Immigrants have come by the millions to partake of America's goodies.  The welcome mat is in place.

    In 1886 the Statue of Liberty, standing 151 feet tall, took her place at America's doorstep beckoning them to come with her invitation:

        Give me your tired, your poor,
        Your huddled masses yearning to breathe free,
        The wretched refuse of your teeming shore,
        Send these, the homeless, tempest-tost to me,

156

I lift my lamp beside the golden door.

It is indeed a golden door for the many millions of immigrants who come to our shores. They are treated extraordinarily well. We lay out the golden platter of goodies.

For centuries not only has our door been open but there are numerous side doors through which many illegal immigrants have crept in.

A substantial number enter legally at airports and other points of entry and overstay their visas.[*] And, so, they have come and continue to come from all over the world.

In Fiscal Year 2000 the United States naturalized 888,788[**] persons. Each year many thousands are naturalized. In 1996 over a million were naturalized.

The number of foreign-born population residing in the United States is estimated at 26,514,715.[***]

Those who enter the United States must do so legally and we should take whatever steps are necessary to ensure that they do.

THE FEDERAL STATUTES provide that an immigrant seeking naturalization must "demonstrate an understanding of the English language, including an ability to read, write, and speak words in ordinary English."

---

[*] SOURCE: U.S. Dept. of **Justice** JOURNAL. Crime & Illegal Immigration **June** 1997
[**] SOURCE: 2001. Statistical Yearbook of the Immigration and Naturalization Service
[***] Bureau of the Census 2000. Excludes 1,864,285 persons who were born abroad of American parents.

*Alice Vaeth*

This is important because communication is basic to human relationships. English must be America's language. Otherwise we are segmenting our country and creating chaos.

Incident to coming to America they should be able to understand and speak commonly used English words and phrases.

It seems that everywhere I go I see instructions and other information printed in Spanish. I'm beginning to wonder if we are no longer America but rather Mexico No. 2, especially since we hear Presidential candidates speaking Spanish in their campaign speeches. In mainstream America, English should be used.

Unless we maintain English as our American language, we may want to rename our country and call it "The Land of Diversity and Chaos."

I believe anyone coming to live in America would want to learn English and we should require that they speak English so they can function as an American. At the present time too many are not functioning as Americans.

All speaking the same language is basic to national unity. And, unity is basic to maintaining peace. We must pursue diligently the speaking of English by all of our citizens.

The FEDERAL STATUTES provide that an immigrant seeking naturalization must "have been a person of good moral character, attached to the principles of the Constitution, and well disposed to the good order and happiness of the United States for 5 years just before filing the petition... and continue to be such a person."

Let's take another look at the words "continue to be such a person." If he doesn't continue to be such a person as regards morality he should be denaturalized and deported to his native land with no possibility of returning and being renaturalized in the future.

Those in elected office or other positions of authority should not be permitted to plead on behalf of those who are denaturalized. A decision by proper authority to denaturalize should be final.

Cultural differences should be confined to religious settings and in the home. In mainstream America there should be only Americanism.

We have witnessed the falling apart of European, Asian, and African nations as they encounter infighting because of diversity. I don't think we want that to happen in America.

In the tiny African nation of Rwanda, about the size of the State of Maryland, the Hutus and the Tutsis couldn't find a common ground on which to keep their nation at peace. The tribes slaughtered each other and many thousands fled to neighboring countries where many died in refugee camps.

In Albania people feared for their lives, suffering killings, rapes, beatings, and destruction of their homes as they fled from their homeland.

The infrastructure and boundaries of nations quiver and fall apart under the pressure of opposing philosophies. They tear at each other with utter inhumanity reflecting disgracefully on what we like to think of as a civilized world.

War has been a part of life since time immemorial and nations topple and rise in its process. There is devastation and warriors march forth to receive medals for their service on the battlefield.

The problem of keeping the peace within nations began in early times. As people multiplied and scattered throughout the world and formed new nations, many clans, tribes, and political enclaves emerged, each with its own culture. Thus, the world has many cultures, each with its own agenda and failing to understand the philosophy of live and let live. Instead, when multiple cultures are compacted within a nation, each seeks to gain superiority and lordship over others.

Let's stand back for a moment and cerebrate on a thought. Do we expect too much of humanity at this stage of civilization? We are still in the embryonic stage of civilization insofar as human relationships are concerned.

Man's inhumanity to man around the world hardly justifies man being labeled as fully civilized. We have a long, long, long way to go. We must forge ahead with civilized objectives. We must strive for harmony. We must seek an end to wars. Possible? Probably not.

Besides our concern about our nation and the world in which we live, we have concerns about our own self as a person. There is the issue on the table about one's control over one's own life.

We travel through life with a body and soul. They are both ours and ours alone. The Government doesn't claim our soul and it has no right to claim our body. They are both ours personally.

Just as the U.S. Constitution provides that there shall be no law respecting an establishment of religion, that is, that each person shall have the right to determine for himself what, if any, religion he wishes for his soul, so it follows that there should be no law respecting man's right to control his own body. Body and soul make the whole person.

For the Government to dictate that someone should bear pain beyond his own willingness and endurance by preventing medical assistance in ending life is holding the suffering person in captivity.

They suffer pain beyond their endurance and they accomplish their death by jumping off a bridge, or however.

About 30,000 persons commit suicide in the United States every year. In addition, an estimated 500,000 people are treated in emergency rooms each year after attempting suicide.[*]

Over the years I have been personally touched by a number of suicides. My son's closest friend committed suicide with a gun on a California university campus. The daughter of a friend of mine, a university student in the middle west, committed suicide by shooting herself in a major department store. A grandson of my doctor, discouraged with life, committed suicide. A son of a colleague of mine committed suicide on a holiday. A doctor, the husband of a friend of mine, committed suicide by hanging himself in the basement of his home. A friend of mine committed suicide by jumping from a high-rise office building.

A lady with whom I worked asked me what I thought about suicide. In the back of my mind I thought she might be contemplating suicide and I wanted to discourage her from doing so. I proceeded to tell her how terrible I think suicide is, that it is wrong, and went on in that vein of thought. She then told me that her father had committed suicide.

I realized immediately how insensitive I had been in my response to her question. We cannot condemn suicide. We must understand it.

We have no right to tell someone suffering beyond their endurance, regardless of what the suffering consists of, as to what they can do with their life. It is their life and their life only.

We are forced into this world. We shouldn't be forced to stay.

Unless we're content with their jumping off bridges and bringing about their demise in other gruesome ways, we should assist them, if they request us to do so, in ending their life in a compassionate way.

---

[*] SOURCE: U.S. Department of Health and Human Services, National Center for Health Statistics.

We may be able to handle the mental and physical problems in our own life, but we must realize that there are those who aren't able to cope, those who are at the end of their ability to tolerate the suffering they bear. It is a cruel government that takes on the control of one's body and dictates that one should live with intolerable suffering.

Common sense tells us that the many thousands who jump off bridges or commit suicide in other gruesome ways would have opted to have a doctor's assistance in bringing about their demise if such assistance were available. The government should be passionate and allow such assistance. Or, does it not concern the government that people jump off bridges or bring about their death in other gruesome ways.

# NOW, SOME FINAL THOUGHTS

During the 20th century we witnessed a great many innovations which have benefited mankind far more than had previously been imagined. But, we haven't done much to better man's treatment of his fellowman. This, we need to work on.

How we conduct ourselves and interact with our fellow human beings during our short stay on this earth has much to do with how much joy of living we ourselves experience.

We should be ever aware of those around us and when we recognize a need we should lend a helping hand. It isn't necessarily a money need. There are many kinds of need to which we can respond.

We must be concerned about the suffering caused by crime. Crime in America is disgraceful. It can be attributed to our system of justice which is antiquated, being centuries old. It doesn't meet today's needs. It doesn't deter crimes.

America gives the criminal tender loving care. This is mandated by the centuries-old Bill of Rights (the first ten Amendments to the U.S. Constitution written centuries ago in 1791). The Bill of Rights could be called the Bill of Sympathy for the Criminal.

Because of the provisions in the Bill of Rights, our justice system looks for every nook and cranny to let the criminal go free. His defense lawyer is part of the problem by hiding detrimental information instead of disclosing whatever knowledge he has about the particular case.

The Bill of Rights provides numerous technical doors to freedom even though the most atrocious crime has been committed. The defense attorney uses these technical doors to obtain freedom for the most hardened criminal. Only one door to freedom should be allowed and that is if it is later found that the person charged with the crime did not commit it.

*Alice Vaeth*

We live in a different world today. America must not continue with an antiquated system of justice that is geared to protecting the criminal instead of protecting the public.

Let's look at the figures and have an understanding of our problem and, furthermore, understand that with so much crime we are not America the land of the free, but rather the land of fear because of so much crime within our borders.

There are about 25,000,000 crimes committed in the United States every year.[*] This reflects disgracefully on America.

The recidivism of prisoners is frightening. In June 2002 the U.S. Department of Justice released the results of a study made of 272,111 prisoners who had been discharged from prison in 1994 in the 15 states it selected for the study.[**]

It found that within 3 years of their release 67.5% of those prisoners were rearrested for a new offense (almost exclusively a felony or a serious misdemeanor). It also found that 46.9% were convicted for a new crime. Within 3 years of release 2.5% of released rapists were rearrested for another rape. And, this was a study of only 15 states. It's frightening.

We should be seriously concerned about all of these crimes but especially about the number of murders and forcible rapes. The victims should be of great concern to America.

We know imprisonment will not reduce crime. We've used it for many years and know it is not an effective answer to our crime problem. The above figures make this very clear. They don't fear prison. It's just a place to live for awhile, a place to join their buddies (think alike) and chat about their experiences, maybe learn some new

---

[*] SOURCE: U.S. Dept. of Justice
[**] SOURCE: U.S. Department of Justice, Office of Justice Programs, Bureau of Justice Statistics, Special Report, NCJ 193427, June 2002

ways to try to get away with crime. The prison library and other prison benefits are there for their enjoyment. Even confinement in a cell is not meaningful punishment. It just sets them apart in another environment for a time. America loves its criminals and takes good care of them. Shame, shame, shame on the Bill of Rights.

Only with physical punishment can we ever hope to reduce crime. And, this should vary according to the nature of the crime. We could start with caning and the number of lashes could vary according to the nature of the crime. Caning would be very mild punishment compared to the brutal crimes that take place.

Without meaningful punishment, punishment that the criminal will fear, we can never rid ourselves of the many horrible crimes committed in America.

Until we rid ourselves of so much horrible crime we have no right to call America the land of the free.

We hope for a time when we will no longer find it necessary to cling tightly to our purses, put double locks on our doors, put bars to our windows, install burglar alarms in our homes, carry protection devices and have metal detection devices installed in public places for security. All of these say shame on America for having a criminal justice system that goes to extremes to protect the criminal and interferes with the happiness of upright American citizens.

We should express our concerns to those who can do something about them. Discussing our concerns at the dinner table with our family, across the fence with neighbors, at a restaurant while having lunch with friends, with our buddies on the golf course, or with our office associates, accomplishes nothing except, perhaps, helping to crystallize our thinking.

Our complaints can all be in vain and accomplish nothing unless they reach the ears of those who are in a position to do something about them, and they are usually none of the above.

The ones who can do something about our concerns and with whom we should register our complaints, requests, etc. are those we elect to office or who hold other positions of authority or responsibility.

We must make sure that those we place in office, elected or otherwise, serve us well. They want to keep their position and know the way to retain their role is to meet the valid needs of the people they serve.

We must go to the polls and exercise our citizenship duty of voting. And, if those we vote in don't do their job the way we think it should be done, the next time around we vote for someone else.

Voting gives us a voice and it is very important that we express our concerns through the voting system.

I urge personal contacts with those who are in a position to do something about complaints, perhaps not an opportunity in person but at least by telephone or correspondence.

Will we...? Will we...? Will we...? Action is needed. Meaningful action. First and foremost to replace the centuries old Bill of Rights which is very outdated for today's world. I cited the figures on crime. You may want to take another look at them. They are very convincing evidence of our need to do something without delay about crime in America.

Our forefathers, in the Preamble to the U.S. Constitution, wrote; "...in Order to form a more perfect Union..." Let's work on updating our justice system to make our country a more perfect Union. Let the first step be to remove those technicalities through which criminals obtain freedom and write a new Bill of Rights.

Finally, confronted with around 25,000,000 crimes committed in the United States every year,[*] it's urgent that we do something about

---

[*] SOURCE: U.S. Dept. of Justice

our failed justice system. The nature of the punishment must be such as will deter crime, otherwise it is meaningless. Also, those on parole or probation should be required to wear something that would identify them as being on parole or probation. I can hear: "Oh, no, we wouldn't do that." That's because there's more concern for the criminal than for the many millions of victims.

Let's take meaningful steps to reduce the number of victims. This is a must for the future of America.

*Alice Vaeth*

# ABOUT THE AUTHOR

Born on Ely Street in Allegan, Michigan, Alice (nee: Lacey) Vaeth lived her growing-up years in Michigan, Indiana, Missouri, and Florida.

Surviving a difficult childhood, at 21 years of age she embarked on a career with the Federal Government in Washington, D.C.

She was praised for her work in the Internal Revenue Service.

She received 6 Awards from the Treasury Department and 3 Honorary Recognition Certificates from the Internal Revenue Service.

She wrote a weekly news column for a local newspaper.

Serious concerns about life, our American justice system and other problems in America prompted the author to write this book. She feels too many problems are being swept under the rug so as not to disturb the image of America.

Alice Vaeth currently resides in the Washington, D.C. area.

Printed in the United States
22936LVS00001B/301

9 781418 426361